A
Cherry Blossom
in the
Dead of Winter

A Memoir by a Chinese *Adopted* American

Autumn Coleman-Marconett

Table of Contents

Prologue

As a little girl, I was mesmerized by cherry blossoms. Their delicate petals, bursting with vibrant pinks and whites, felt magical against the backdrop of a world still shaking off the cold of winter. I would twirl under their branches, letting their delicate petals brush against my cheeks, believing they carried whispers of hope and new beginnings.

Back then, I did not realize just what these flowers would come to mean to me. As the years passed and my own wisdom grew, I turned the lens of contemplation upon the mosaic of my own life. The plants I once admired with idle delight underwent a metamorphosis in my perception. No longer were they mere ornaments of nature, pleasing to the eye yet detached from my inner world; they became a symbol of my unspoken fortitude and steadfast determination. I now see that these are the qualities that undergird my very being.

Like cherry blossom roots burrowed deep into the earth, unseen yet essential for the health of the tree, my own origins had anchored me. I was drawing strength from hidden reservoirs without even realizing it. These roots are what formed the architecture of my survival.

I used to see cherry blossoms as only a burst of spring's beauty: fragile, beautiful, and happy in the warm sun. But then I realized that these were plants that endured through the winter, gathering strength, adapting, until it was time for them to bloom once more. In their fleeting bloom, I saw my own reflection: that the rarest beauty is often born of hardship, that endurance refines rather than diminishes.

You could say I identify as a cherry blossom. I was born into hardship, my life shaped by challenges from the very beginning. Yet, even in the face of adversity, my path felt clear. I carried a sense of honor, loyalty, and purpose. From an early age, I knew who I was meant to be, as if something inside me refused to let my struggles define me. Every obstacle became a test, proof that my beginning, no matter how difficult, would not determine my worth. Instead, it became the foundation for something greater. Those would be my roots. Aspects of me fused with the earth where I came from, now so strong that they could help me flourish when my season arrived.

The most challenging season of my life was my teenage years. During this time, my journey shifted toward seeking acceptance from the outside world, abandoning my innate spirit, and going against what I had yet to understand was the truth of my own being. I yearned to find my place in society or within a peer group, wanting to feel that my very existence was accepted unconditionally.

As I entered young adulthood, my path took another turn, this time toward self-discovery. My emotions conflicted with the truths I knew about my past, pulling me in different directions and often leaving me feeling stuck in the present.

Now, as I sit in reflection, I see a path marked by turbulence, chaos, and a relentless push toward an end goal, one that left the story of how I came to be buried in the dust where I thought it belonged. But those pivotal seasons of life, each featuring its own battles and breakthroughs, have shaped a deeper understanding: self-acceptance.

I hope that by sharing my story, I can spark something within you: an itch for self-discovery, a sense of peace in your own journey, and the courage to embrace who you were, who you are, and who you are still becoming. Life is a balance of struggles and achievements, and I have learned that both are worth welcoming. Every challenge, every success, and every moment in between has shaped me into the person I am today.

I am a Chinese-born, American-raised adoptee. My story is one of strength, growth, and the power of truly knowing oneself.

Chapter 1:
Cherry Blossoms

I was born in January, a month that symbolizes fresh beginnings and endless possibilities. The start of a new year brings renewal, a season when hope runs high and the promise of great opportunities feels within reach. People make resolutions and set ambitions, a collective excitement spreading across North America, inspiring many to chase dreams and embrace change.

In China, however, the new year carries a different meaning. It is a time of reflection, a moment to look back on the past year, to honor victories that brought joy, cherish memories that warmed the heart, and acknowledge losses that left their mark. It is a season of remembrance and of hope for peace, prosperity, and better days ahead. Though these traditions differ, they share a universal truth: every new year holds both the weight of the past and the promise of the future.

My story began, like everyone's, at birth, in the year 1996. For the United States, the 1990s were a decade marked by peace and prosperity. The internet was emerging as a revolutionary force, reshaping how businesses communicated and transforming the entertainment industry. Fashion shifted away from the bold, intricate styles of the 1980s toward a more minimalist aesthetic, yet with hints of the 1970s subtly woven in.

On the world stage, history was in transition. The fall of the Soviet Union ended the decades-long Cold War, reshaping global politics and ushering in a new era of international relations. Yet the 1990s were also marked by tragedy: the Rodney King beating and the resulting L.A. Riots, the Columbine High School shooting, the Oklahoma City bombing, and the first World Trade Center bombing, each one shaking the American sense of security.

In China, the decade was equally pivotal. Following the 1989 Tiananmen Square protests and massacre, Deng Xiaoping stepped down from his role, leaving Jiang Zemin as the Chinese Communist Party's leader. The global condemnation that followed Tiananmen strained China's reputation and its relations with the United States. The U.S. Congress pressed for economic sanctions, canceled cultural exchanges, and sought to restrict trade. Despite this, President George H.W. Bush maintained that the difficulties were temporary and that Sino-U.S. relations would recover.

Yet beneath the political turbulence, China was rebuilding. Economic growth and stability became national priorities. High fashion mirrored global trends, with luxury and exclusivity seen as aspirational goals. Designer labels became symbols of success. In the early 1990s, shoulder-padded women's suits reflected both power and sophistication, representing women's growing role in our social fabric.

You might be thinking, "Why am I getting a lesson in geopolitics while reading a memoir?" My intent in sharing this is not to give you a history lesson but to paint the backdrop of my birth: two nations, both very different, on two sides of the globe, both in transition, whose macro politics would ripple through the waters of my own microcosm of a life.

One of the most defining realities of my birth year was China's One-Child Policy. Though introduced in the late 1970s and early 1980s, its impact was deeply felt in my generation. The policy, designed to slow population growth, limited most families to a single child. It was meant to ease economic and social pressures, but its consequences shaped family structures, cultural expectations, and the destinies of countless children, mine included.

When the People's Republic of China was established in 1949, the government encouraged birth control and family planning, though early efforts were voluntary. Under Deng Xiaoping's leadership, population control became a central focus. The initial limit was two children, but soon, pressure mounted for a stricter one-child rule, which was unevenly enforced across provinces.

By 1980, the policy became nationwide. Urban families were more likely to comply, while rural areas saw more flexibility. Compliance was ensured through a mix of incentives, such as financial rewards and job advantages, and punishments, including fines and loss of benefits. The most harrowing measures were forced abortions and sterilizations, which left physical and emotional scars on women across the country.

With the policy still active in 1996, the circumstances of my birth raise questions that may never have answers. But one possibility is painfully simple: I was a girl.

In Chinese tradition, sons have long been valued over daughters. This preference, reflected in the sex ratio at birth (SRB), is rooted largely in economics. Sons are expected to provide for their parents in old age, while daughters marry into their husband's family. In rural, agricultural communities, this bias was even stronger; farming was considered a man's work, and sons were seen as essential for labor and legacy.

Under the One-Child Policy, this cultural preference magnified the disparity: orphanages became filled with more girls than boys. I was not the first, nor the last, little girl to be born into this social reality. I was one of thousands, a drop in the ocean; my life expectancy in the eyes of society was reduced to something short and grim.

Nanjing, the capital of Jiangsu Province in eastern China, sits in the province's southwestern corner and is made up of eleven districts. With its rich and storied past, the city holds a prominent place in Chinese history and culture. Over the centuries, it has served as the capital for various dynasties, republican governments, and kingdoms, its political significance stretching from as early as the 3rd century up until 1949.

Because of its deep historical roots, Nanjing has become a major hub for culture, education, research, politics, the economy, transportation, and tourism. Known as the "capital of the Ten Dynasties," it boasts an abundance of historical relics and lies within the Yangtze River Delta, one of China's largest and most important economic zones. Positioned in the heart of the drainage area of the Yangtze's lower reaches and the Yangtze River Delta, the city thrives at the meeting point of history and modernity.

The bridges and tunnels spanning the Yangtze River connect road and rail networks across China's longest and largest river, forming a vital artery in the country's transportation infrastructure. The river itself slices across China from west to east, and every major north–south highway and railway must cross it.

Four months after my birth, on May 29, 1996, a police officer found me near the Yangtze River Bridge. Pinned to me was a small, carefully written note stating my birthdate and the exact time I was born, one of the only tangible traces of my beginnings. With no way to locate my parents, the officer brought me to the Nanjing Children's Welfare Institution, where I would spend my earliest years waiting for a fate yet to unfold.

I was declared legally eligible for adoption and given the name **Qiu Xianqiu**, meaning "Earlier Autumn." Like the season it evoked, the name carried both an ending and the promise of a new beginning.

The Nanjing Children's Welfare Institution, established in 1951 and located today in Hou Zai Men Village, was very different in the 1990s from what it is now. While care for orphans has improved greatly over the years, the orphanage during my time there was far from ideal. Because of the One-Child Policy, abandonment was common, and orphanages became overcrowded. Most of the children left behind were girls, not because they were unloved, but because societal rules and expectations made it difficult, sometimes impossible, for families to keep them.

Overcrowding and understaffing made even basic care a challenge. It was common for two or even three children to share a single crib. Food was scarce, and there was little to no functioning heating or cooling. Extreme weather, combined with food shortages, claimed many young lives.

For most of my time there, I was told I shared a crib with another child. When the time came for my U.S. travel visa physical, the reality of my condition was clear. Just six days before my first birthday, I weighed a little over fourteen pounds and measured 27.5 inches, far below the 50th percentile for baby girls in the United States. I was malnourished, fragile, and yet standing unknowingly on the brink of a life-changing journey.

One of the reasons why the babies in the orphanage were so unhealthy was the struggle to keep the building warm, which led workers to layer multiple blankets over the children, securing them tightly to preserve what heat they could. Though done with the intent to protect us, this was not enough. Some children did not survive the cold.

There was a slew of other health issues caused by the poor conditions in the orphanages. When I arrived in the United States, I needed corrective shoes to reshape my feet. The weight of those tightly bound blankets had pressed them downward and inward, affecting their natural growth. Even today, I can fold my feet completely parallel, one atop the other, a lasting imprint of those early days.

One would think that life could only improve from there. But as the years passed, I came to realize that the past is never something you simply leave behind. It lives within you, shaping you in ways you might not understand until much later.

Chapter 2:
Pink Dresses

Halfway across the globe, in the heart of the Midwest, a couple was building a life together in the growing community of Johnson County, Kansas. Dan and Patricia Coleman were, in many ways, a picture of the American dream, rooted in tradition, family, and love. Both were born and raised in the Midwest. They found each other, fell in love, and married on July 17th, 1992. Dan Coleman, born to Donald and Georgia Coleman in November 1961, carries a kind of strength that came from generations of Midwestern bravery. Patricia Coleman (Marrinaeu), born to Charles and Florence Marrinaeu in October 1961, had a warmth in herself. She had a nurturing spirit, largely due to the responsibility of raising three biological children before she even met Dan. Life for them was, as you would imagine, with three small children. Their home was filled with laughter, love, and the occasional mess, but something told them their family wasn't quite complete yet; they had more love to give.

Dan worked at Time Warner Cable Company, and Patricia (Trish) worked in an in-home daycare. They lived a quaint life with three small kids, which was lively and full. Their four-bedroom, two-bathroom home in the suburbs rang with laughter, love, and the occasional chaos. Still, they both sensed their family wasn't quite complete. They had more love to give.

One day, while Trish was watching *Life Today with James Robison*, the conversation turned to China. Something in her stirred. A long-buried memory surfaced: as a little girl, she once told her cousin she would have children of her own and adopt others someday, a promise she didn't realize was rooted in her own story. She would later discover, only after adopting her daughter, that she herself had been adopted.

The feeling grew stronger. Excited and a little nervous, Trish decided to share it with Dan.

When she brought up the idea of adopting, her voice was full of hope. Dan listened, his face unreadable. After a pause, he finally said, "Only rich people adopt children." The words landed heavy. Trish knew he wasn't wrong; adoption was expensive, and they didn't have the extra resources. But she met his eyes and replied softly, "To them, we are rich." Dan said nothing more, and Trish let the conversation rest, trusting that if this was meant to be, God would change his heart.

Weeks passed. The topic faded, but the feeling in Trish's heart didn't. Unknown to her, something was shifting in Dan as well. Though he had dismissed the idea at first, he began noticing small, persistent reminders, news stories, TV segments, and radio broadcasts, all about China. He brushed them off at first, telling himself they already had enough with the three children they were raising together. Adoption still felt impossible.

One morning, they went to breakfast at the Village Inn in downtown Merriam, a cozy, well-worn diner that felt like part of the neighborhood's heartbeat. They slid into a booth near the entrance, chatting casually over pancakes and tea. Halfway through the meal, Trish noticed Dan set his fork down. His steady eyes held something new, something unspoken. Dan wasn't a man to waste words, and she knew when he spoke next, it would matter.

"I think we should adopt a baby from China," he said.

Trish froze, stunned. They hadn't spoken of adoption since the first conversation, and now here it was, spoken into the air as if it had always been inevitable. She immediately began to cry into her pancakes. Dan explained that everywhere he turned, the TV, the newspaper, and the radio, China was there. It felt like God was speaking to him. In that little booth, over an ordinary breakfast, they decided to become my mom and dad.

From there, the research began. At the time, international adoption, especially from China, was still far from the norm. Most adoptions were domestic, from the foster care system. The process ahead was neither simple nor clearly mapped. But through Hand in Hand Adoptions, Dan and Trish found a guide for the journey.

Excited but anxious, they began preparing for what lay ahead: extensive background checks, home visits, personal interviews, and approvals from both the U.S. and China. Their only request was that the child be a baby girl. They saved and documented every dollar needed, not only for adoption fees but also for flights, hotels, passports, and other costs.

A little over a year later, the day finally came. The day my parents would see my face for the first time.

Trish knew the package was coming and paced the house in anticipation. When the doorbell rang, she practically snatched the FedEx envelope from the delivery driver's hands. She tore it open and pulled out a small photograph.

The baby in the picture had short black hair, dark brown eyes so deep they were almost black, and round red cheeks that seemed to take up half her face. That baby was me.

Tears streamed down her face as a rush of emotions crashed over her. Every hardship of the journey flashed before her: endless paperwork, long nights of waiting, and the fragile hope that had carried her here. But above all, she thought of the little girl whose face now looked back at her from the photograph. And then, another woman entered her mind, the mother who had carried this child, who had looked into those same dark eyes, and made the impossible choice to walk away. The weight of that sacrifice made her tears fall harder.

With trembling hands, she took the photo to the store to have it enlarged, wanting to see every detail, every tiny feature that made this child real. Clutching the image, she rushed to her daughter's school, where the class happened to be learning about different countries. As the teacher began speaking about China, she seized her moment. Holding up the photo, the teacher announced, "Oh look! Here is a picture of Brooke's little sister."

For a moment, there was silence. Then Brooke, my sister, sprang from her seat and ran to look at the photo. Her eyes, glistening with tears, locked onto the baby's face. She knew instantly: this was her little sister.

Later that day, when my dad came home from work, he slipped into his usual routine, settling into his recliner with a cup of coffee and the evening newspaper. But as he lifted the paper, a small photograph slid down into view. He looked up to see my mom standing there, eyes red and brimming with anticipation. He studied the picture, his gaze lingering on the round cheeks and dark eyes. It wasn't just any baby. It was his daughter. His eyes welled as he looked back at my mom, and without a single word, they both knew this was the child they had been waiting for.

From that moment, preparations began in earnest. The nursery became a dreamscape, with freshly painted white walls softened with blush pink accents, sturdy wooden furniture with gleaming gold handles, and rows of plush toys and dolls waiting patiently for tiny hands to hold them. The closet was filled with tiny dresses, onesies, and shoes, each piece carefully hung as though guarding the perfection of the moment they had imagined for so long. By the door, the suitcases sat ready, packed with clothes, diapers, toys, and love, so much love, waiting to be carried halfway across the world.

When it was time to leave, they said their goodbyes. My mom kissed her children and promised to return soon with their new baby sister. Grandma Coleman joined them for the journey. As they drove to the airport, familiar scenery passed by: the trees, the lawns, the quiet streets of Kansas, each mile bringing them closer to a life forever changed.

The flight carried them 7,000 miles across the Pacific Ocean. When they landed, it was into a whirlwind of sights and sounds. China was alive with motion, taxis darting, bicycles weaving through traffic, and scooters stacked high with goods and families riding together. The air was thick with the scent of street food and the hum of a city always on the move. Vendors called out over the clamor, eager to be heard.

My mother gazed out over the bustling streets, a lump rising in her throat. Was someone here connected to her baby? A birth parent, a relative, someone who had once held her? The thought broke her open, and tears welled again. This was her child's first home, rich with history, love, and loss.

As they walked, she began to notice the stares. People paused mid-step, stopping their bicycles to look. Some reached out to touch her golden-blonde curls, speaking softly to one another about the striking pair before them, my tall, dark-haired father standing beside her, his 6'5" frame making her look even smaller. They were an unusual sight here, opposites that somehow fit together perfectly.

They explored the city, my dad recalling his Navy travels while my mom took in her first overseas adventure. They greeted strangers, sampled new foods, and marveled at the world around them. But no matter where they went or what they saw, one thought never left their minds: When would they finally hold their baby?

The time had finally come. My parents waited anxiously in the hotel, knowing that at any moment, the babies would arrive. They had been told the women would come, each carrying a child in their arms. There is video footage of my dad pacing back and forth, his hands tightly clasped together. He wore a path in the carpet from his constant pacing, the anticipation practically radiating off him.

They weren't alone; other couples from the adoption agency were there too, most from Colorado, where the agency was based. The room was filled with quiet chatter from the women and tense, eager glances from the men. Then, in the distance, a row of women began to appear, each carrying a baby.

One by one, the women stepped forward and gently placed each baby on a hotel bed. Their hands were careful, but there was a tremor in their movements. Slowly, with practiced yet reverent gestures, they began removing the babies' layers of clothing. As each soft layer fell away, the babies' delicate frames were revealed, the tiny limbs, the small hands, and the fragile beauty of each child.

The room was hushed, thick with anticipation. The parents didn't need to be told which baby was theirs; they had memorized every feature from photographs, tracing those faces in their dreams for months. As the final layers came off, eyes welled with tears of recognition. This was the moment they had been waiting for: the moment they finally met their child.

One by one, parents stepped forward to receive their babies. The caregivers would meet them halfway, gently placing the child into their arms. My mother watched impatiently until she saw me being placed on the bed. As my layers came off, she stared at me in awe, her eyes already filled with tears. When she heard my name, she bolted forward.

The young Chinese woman who held me smiled warmly. With both care and love, she handed me into my mother's waiting arms. In that instant, when our eyes met, my mother felt a familiar surge of emotion. She had felt it only once before: the indescribable moment when a newborn is placed on a mother's chest. The room faded. The noise disappeared. It was just the two of us, locked in that perfect moment.

She studied my face, memorizing every feature, every tiny movement. And as I looked back at her, she saw everything, every tear shed, every sleepless night, every whispered prayer, reflected in my eyes. In that moment, she felt whole.

Yet, as she held me, she was thinking not only of the life ahead but also of the woman who had brought me into the world. She thought of the mother whose features I bore, the mother who had made the most heartbreaking choice a parent can make. Her joy was deep, but so was her awareness that it came from another's loss. Later, she often wondered: Does her bio mom still think about her baby? Does she picture what kind of life her child has now?

I had no idea that this woman in white, the one holding me so tightly, would one day be "Mom." All I knew was that I didn't like it when she handed me to my dad. I fussed when she held me, but when my dad took me, I screamed even louder. My dad's deep voice startled me so much that he later had to adopt a high-pitched "Mickey Mouse" voice just to soothe me.

As the commotion settled, the caregivers gathered the clothes we had arrived in and returned to the orphanage. The new parents clung to their babies, speaking softly through tears, while the babies, unfamiliar with these new faces, wailed in confusion. It was a chaotic, emotional scene none of us actually remembered, but one that shaped the rest of our lives.

We stayed in Nanjing for a few more days, visiting places that were now part of my story. One stop was the Yangtze River Bridge, the very spot where I had been found. My family stood quietly, taking in the weight of the moment. Nearby, we wandered into a small gift shop. The shopkeepers immediately noticed me and began speaking excitedly in Mandarin.

Though my mom was hesitant, she handed me over to one of the women to be polite. The woman smiled, touching my tiny hands and cheeks, calling me beautiful. Then, without warning, they carried me into a back room. My mom's heart pounded as the seconds stretched into what felt like hours. Just as she was about to panic, they returned, smiling, and handed me back.

Over the years, my mom would sometimes wonder if they had recognized me. Maybe they were checking to be sure. Maybe they saw something familiar they didn't say aloud. It's a question we'll never truly have an answer to.

From Nanjing, we traveled to Guangzhou to stay at the well-known White Swan Hotel, where the adoption would be finalized. Every adopted child who stayed there received a special Barbie doll, a blonde woman holding an Asian baby.

Back in the hotel room, my mom never put me down. For the first time in my life, I had undivided attention and affection, and I wasn't about to let it go. I was practically attached to her hip, and even a simple trip to the bathroom wasn't happening without me by her side. For the first time, I felt safe, and I wasn't letting go.

As our time in China drew to a close, they decided to go out to dinner as a family to celebrate before parting ways. My adoption had taken place just six days before my first birthday, and my mom had packed a light pink lace dress especially for the occasion. The other little girls wore traditional Chinese red, a color that symbolizes luck and happiness.

We were lined up together on a couch for a group picture, a snapshot of the very beginning of our lives together. And there I was, right in the middle, the only one in pink. At the time, it didn't seem significant. We had been placed there without thought, just a photographer's quick arrangement. But looking back, it feels special, almost as if it had been meant to be.

That first picture became more than just a photograph. Over the years, when we adoptees met again, without realizing it, we would always sit in that exact same order, just as we had the first time. Some connections are like that, natural, unplanned, and somehow inevitable.

When it was time to leave, my parents carefully packed their bags, tucking clothes alongside souvenirs they had collected during the trip. As always, they returned with far more than they had brought, both in belongings and in memories. And, of course, one of those "things" was me.

The final leg of our journey home began with the long flight from China to the United States in January 1997. To anyone who happened to be on that plane, I would like to apologize. In retrospect, I was not an easy seatmate. But I hope you do not blame me; my world had been turned upside down, and I didn't know how to handle all the changes. My mom had packed ten extra outfits for me, and I managed to go through every single one before we landed. Plus, my usual formula had been unavailable, and the substitute did not sit well with my stomach. Let's just say… neither of us was winning that battle.

By the time we landed, a crowd of family and friends had gathered at the airport to welcome us home. For them, it was a joyful, long-awaited moment, but for me, it was overwhelming. New faces, loud voices, unfamiliar smells, I did the only thing I knew how to do: cry at the top of my lungs.

And then, something shifted. I noticed everyone watching me. A little thought crossed my mind: Was I the center of attention? It sure felt like it. And I had a sneaking suspicion it wouldn't be the last time.

Through the chaos, my siblings beamed at me. Their smiles were wide, their eyes bright; they were finally meeting their new little sister. Hugs were exchanged, laughter echoed, and there were a few tears, too, but the happy kind. Even though my stomach was still uneasy, I could feel it: I was safe. I was loved. I was home.

It wasn't long before my new family decided to throw a party, not just for my first birthday, but to celebrate my adoption. Friends and relatives filled the room, eager to meet me. The theme? Pandas, of course. My cake was decorated with an adorable panda face, and when I took my first bite, my eyes widened in wonder. By the end of the night, I was covered in black frosting, grinning from ear to ear.

That day marked more than just turning one year old. It was the beginning of countless celebrations to come, because I had received the greatest gift of all, my forever family.

Chapter 3:
Fish and Crackers

I have carried many names throughout my life: daughter, sister, wife, and mother. Each one has shaped me in its own way, leaving behind layers of meaning and responsibility. But the name that means the most to me, the one I hold closest to my heart, is the name I was given the day I was adopted.

My name is Autumn Danielle Coleman. I am the daughter of Dan and Patricia Coleman. I have three older siblings whom I deeply admire and respect. For most people, a name is simply something given at birth, a label that follows them without much thought. But for me, my name is far more than that. It is the one thing in my life that has always been truly mine.

For as long as I can remember, I have had to share. At the orphanage, I shared a crib. Later, I shared my parents, my home, my space, and sometimes even my sense of belonging. It often felt as though nothing belonged solely to me. But that changed the day I was given my name. That was the moment I finally held something that was mine and mine alone.

Yes, there are others in the world with the first name Autumn, but the story behind mine is unique. The orphanage had given me a Chinese name, and when my parents adopted me, they decided to honor that heritage. They named me Autumn, the English translation. You could say my name was the only thing I carried with me from China to the United States. And no matter what, I will never change it, even though people still manage to get it wrong. I've been called every season, mistaken for Fall, April, and even "Atom," the smallest unit of matter.

For a few fleeting months each year, my name is everywhere, printed on decorations, signs, and shop displays. But for the rest of the year, it disappears. You won't find it on keychains or souvenirs at a gas station. It's not common, and that's exactly what makes it special. My name is uniquely mine, and I will always cherish it.

Life as a baby and toddler was simple, yet profoundly precious. Most days were filled with bottles, cuddles, and the joy of discovering what my little body could do. I was the center of my family's world, the baby they had so longed for. My older siblings, Geoffrey (or "Geoff"), Natalie, and Brooke, welcomed me with open arms. My parents poured themselves into giving me everything I had been without for so long.

They knew how fragile the early years were. An infant's first year is said to be the most important, with ages two to five shaping much of who we become. Because of the way I entered the world, my parents were especially mindful of my milestones, determined that I would not fall behind. Thankfully, I was a fast learner. The basics, walking, talking, and everything in between, came naturally to me.

For a time, I spoke both Chinese and English fluently. But because Chinese was rarely spoken around me, it slowly faded away until it slipped from my grasp. There were moments when I stumbled backward, experiencing some childhood regression, but I always found my way forward again.

One memory, though not my own, has lived with me and really changed how I see myself. My older sister was the one to tell me about this event, and she, too, has never forgotten it. She told me that whenever I cried as a baby, my cries didn't sound like ordinary baby cries. They carried something deeper, an ache, a sorrow too heavy for someone so small. She said her heart would break each time she heard me, and she rushed to soothe me, usually with a bottle. She believed that even though I was so small, I knew that I had to cry to survive. I knew that crying was the way to bring attention to myself and get what I needed. The way she describes it makes me realize that even as an infant, I knew that what was happening to me was not usual, that I was in a foreign place with people who were not my blood.

Still, I adjusted to my family quickly. Though most of my early memories are fuzzy, I know in my heart what I felt during that time. I have always struggled with this feeling of not fully knowing where I belong. As I grew older, my actions and emotions made it clear that I was settling in, becoming just another American kid.

When I officially became a U.S. citizen, we celebrated in the most American way possible. I wore a little sailor dress, and we went to McDonald's for lunch. Looking back, that image makes me smile. It seems fitting that something so monumental was celebrated in such an ordinary way.

This process had been difficult because the law hadn't changed yet. At the time, internationally adopted children were not automatically granted U.S. citizenship even if their parents were American. I had to go through the formal naturalization process. It was just another step in my journey of belonging, a way to anchor me legally to the family I was already bound to by love. That is why, tucked safely away, I still keep my Certificate of Citizenship.

Certain memories from my toddler years remain vivid. I remember being about three years old, sitting on the floor of the family room, carefully working on a puzzle. My mother had stepped out to run errands, leaving my father in charge. He leaned down and asked me to stay put, to promise that I wouldn't do anything I wasn't supposed to. I wanted to be good, so I said "yes."

But soon after our little exchange, he fell asleep, as he often did when left in charge. He stretched out on the couch, arms crossed over his chest, his hands tucked into his armpits. He was such a tall man that no couch ever seemed big enough to hold him comfortably. Even now, that memory makes me smile. It reminds me of the trust between us, of the innocence of that moment, and of how even small details can stay imprinted on a child's heart.

It was in that moment that I broke my very first promise.

I had sworn to my dad that I would stay put, but sitting there alone with a puzzle quickly became unbearable. The house was so quiet, so empty of people, and boredom has always been a dangerous companion for a child. I stood up and began to wander, looking for trouble without realizing that's exactly what I would find.

In the kitchen, I stumbled upon my first discovery: a black marker. Not just any marker, a permanent one. My mind lit up with the kind of "brilliant" idea only a child could have. I would draw a special picture for my parents. The problem was that I couldn't find any paper or crayons. And then it struck me: why make them search for my artwork when I could surprise my mom by drawing it directly on the fridge? That way, she wouldn't even have to hang it up. My masterpiece would already be on display, right in the heart of our home.

I dragged a dining room chair across the floor, climbed up with determination, and went to work. Soon, I grew restless again. My eyes wandered and landed on two clear bottles sitting on the counter. I thought of our pet cat. "Oh yes," I told myself, "the cat must need water." Somehow, I managed to open them and poured the contents into the cat's dish. To this day, I still wonder how I even managed to twist those caps off.

But once the mission was complete, I was again in search of something new to conquer. That's when I passed through the dining room and saw the one thing that always captured my attention: the giant fish tank. It stood like a glowing world against the wall, almost beckoning to me.

My mother's voice echoed in my head, as it often did when I looked at the tank. She would talk about how sometimes the fish would pick on each other, biting tails and bullying the weaker ones. I remembered her once saying that if they didn't stop, she would "take care of them."

In my child's mind, that was all the permission I needed. A wonderful idea bloomed: I could be the hero. I could take care of the bullies myself and earn my mom's praise.

I knew it wouldn't be easy. Even my mom, with all her patience, sometimes struggled to catch the fish when she cleaned the tank. But I was determined. I dragged a wooden chair into position, climbed up, and armed myself with the small green net. I scattered food into the water, watching as the fish eagerly gathered. That was my chance. One by one, I scooped them out, each catch filling me with pride. I felt brilliant, smarter even than my mom, for thinking of such a simple trick.

But catching one fish wasn't enough. I kept going, so caught up in the thrill that soon I had netted them all. I ran into the kitchen, grabbed a flimsy sandwich bag, the kind you fold over instead of sealing, and filled it with my slippery prizes. The bag sagged in my little hands as I clutched it tight. I felt so proud of myself.

Now came the final step. Where to put them? My eyes darted toward the bathroom. That felt right. It was a place of disposal, a place where things went away. Without hesitation, I carried my bag of fish inside, closed the door behind me, and held the bag over the toilet. I stared at them, pressed together in that small, suffocating space, still swimming in circles. My curiosity rose. Where would they go? Would they find a new home somewhere down the pipes? Years later, when I saw *Finding Nemo*, I would laugh at the thought that maybe they had adventures of their own.

Just then, I heard it, the heavy footsteps of my father moving across the living room floor, calling my name. My heart raced. Panic rushed over me. He stopped outside the bathroom door.

"Autumn?" he called.

"I'm going to the bathroom," I quickly answered, trying to steady my voice.

"Okay, it's time for bed," he replied. Relief washed over me, but I knew I didn't have long.

I whispered a little prayer for the fish, closed my eyes, and let the bag slip into the toilet bowl. Without watching, without waiting, I flushed. It was over in seconds.

I opened the bathroom door and hurried out to find my dad.

Looking back now, I see so much more than just mischief in that memory. I see a child's longing for approval, for control, for a chance to prove herself worthy of love. I see the beginnings of my creativity, unrestrained, bold, but also reckless. And I see how even small promises, once broken, can leave a mark that lingers long after childhood fades.

We walked up the stairs together to my bedroom, which sat just at the top on the left. I changed into my pajamas, feeling completely worn out from the day, but also proud of myself. I thought I had done a good job helping my mom that evening.

A little later, she came home carrying bags of groceries. She walked right past the fish tank without even glancing at it, heading straight into the kitchen to set everything down on the counter. As she began putting things away, she suddenly remembered the fish needed to be fed. Turning back toward the living room, she stopped dead in her tracks.

There, on top of the tank, lay the wet green fishnet. A small puddle had formed beneath it, spreading across the surface like a clue to some hidden crime. She peered into the tank and froze. No fish. Not a single one. Confusion crossed her face. Where had they gone?

Then she spotted something else: two empty bottles sitting on the counter. Panic surged through her. She immediately thought I had drunk the medicine. Abandoning everything, she bolted up the stairs, rushed into my room, and shook me awake.

Groggy, I rubbed my eyes, still half-asleep. She asked sharply if I had drunk the bottles. I barely understood the words. She repeated the question, her urgency rising. I shook my head no. Then she pressed harder, asking where the liquid had gone. When I didn't answer quickly enough, she made me get up and show her.

I slowly guided her back downstairs to the kitchen and pointed to the cat's dish. She bent over, sniffed, and saw the liquid pooled on both sides of the bowl. Relief and fresh worry collided across her face. At least I hadn't overdosed, but now she feared the cat had.

Once that fear passed, her attention turned back to the missing fish. She marched me into the living room, eyes narrowing at the empty tank. "Where are the fish?" she demanded.

I stood frozen, two warring thoughts in my mind: should I tell the truth or blame my dad? She glared at me. Finally, instead of answering, I turned and walked toward the hallway bathroom. Stopping in front of the toilet, I slowly pointed at it.

Her eyes followed my hand, and in an instant, realization dawned. The look on her face made my heart drop. At that moment, I was fairly certain I was about to meet Jesus. I couldn't understand why she was so upset. In my child's mind, I thought she would be proud; after all, I had "fixed" the problem of the fish fighting.

The rest of that night is a blur. I don't remember the punishment, only the weight of her disappointment and the storm brewing between my parents. I can still imagine her confronting my dad, asking where he had been while all this unfolded. And his classic responses: "What? Me? No way!" or the playful, "I didn't fall asleep; I just watched the TV behind my eyelids. Every time I startled awake, she was still there." My mom, unimpressed, would roll her eyes and demand he do better. But that was usually the end of it.

If anyone should've "met Jesus" that night, it was probably him, not me.

To make matters worse, my mom often reminded us that those fish were expensive. You'd think that both my dad and I would have learned our lesson: me for wandering, and him for napping. But the truth is, we didn't.

Another classic "Autumn story" came not long after, the time I almost blew up the house.

I don't remember it firsthand, but my mom has told the story so many times it feels etched in my own memory. It was extremely early in the morning when she woke to find me standing beside her bed, breathing heavily as if I had just run a marathon, clutching something tightly in my little hand.

Her eyes adjusted to the dim light as I proudly announced, "Mommy, I got goldfish cackas."

Half-asleep, she blinked at me, trying to make sense of what I was saying. I repeated myself, "I got goldfish cackas."

Still groggy, she finally asked, "Oh? Where did you get those Goldfish crackers?" with interest in her voice mixed with the feeling as if she didn't want to know.

Without hesitation, I replied, "Downstairs." Curious and perhaps a little concerned, she sat up and motioned for me to show her exactly how I had obtained them. As we made our way down the stairs through the living room and dining room, she came to the entrance of the kitchen. I beamed with joy, thinking I had achieved greatness. Suddenly, her nose caught a whiff of gas filling the room. She swiftly moved to the stove, which was positioned to her left, next to the fridge. She, without hesitation, turned off the gas switch. She then saw the pan teetering on the stove, the silverware drawer open, the cabinet door ajar, and the bag of Goldfish crackers spilling out onto the counter.

It was like a scene from the movie "Home Alone" after Kevin made his ice cream, with the camera slowly panning through the kitchen to show the dripping ice cream and open candy containers, all looking like a giant sticky mess on the counter. But you can see what was happening. She looked at me, and I smiled excitedly, proud of my independence. She was happy that I felt like I could come to her and tell her about my little adventure. Otherwise, we probably wouldn't be here today. So, honestly, I see that as a positive. After this, I was officially locked in my room at night until morning when she came to wake me. By locked, I mean there was a small metal hook too high for me to reach, which I'd hook into the latch on the doorframe. This was before safety items like plastic door handle covers, which could only be opened by adults, were invented.

Looking back, I see these stories not only as misadventures but also as glimpses into the essence of who I was: curious, bold, imaginative, and endlessly determined.

When I was four, my parents decided it was time to adopt again. This time, they wanted to adopt a little boy, ideally around three years old or older, from Thailand. They hoped that having a sibling close to my age and also adopted would give me someone to relate to. My older siblings often spent time at their dad's house, leaving me alone without playmates until they returned. Plus, my dad had always dreamed of having a son.

I remember feeling conflicted. On one hand, I enjoyed being the center of attention, the one everyone doted on. On the other hand, the thought of having a built-in playmate was appealing.

In July of 2000, Eric joined our family at three years old from Chiang Mai, Thailand. From that moment on, he became both my forever best friend and my fiercest rival. Our sibling rivalry ran deep. We could play well together, but nine times out of ten, those moments of peace led to mischief. And somehow, Eric always took the blame.

Eric took over my old bedroom at the top of the stairs, while I moved to a room across from my older sister's on the main floor. To ease the transition and help me feel less "replaced," my mom decided to remodel my room around my panda obsession. The walls were painted tan, the bedding featured pandas and stalks of bamboo, and the accents matched the theme. The highlight was the mural my mom painted herself: two pandas, one hunched over a log, the other perched in a tree, with snowcapped purple mountains in the background. She was, and still is, an incredibly talented artist. Eric's room, in contrast, was decorated with Dalmatians, from bedding to wallpaper.

Around this time, my dad switched jobs, leaving Time Warner Cable to become a railroad engineer with BNSF Railway. As a little girl, I liked to think I was the reason he got the job. I had helped him practice railroad crossing hand signals for his engineer test over and over again. When he passed, I was bursting with pride, convinced it was because of me. He even had me demonstrate the signals at a meeting shortly after being hired. I can still picture the giant, muscular men chuckling as they watched this tiny little girl waving her arms with intensity and seriousness.

While my dad transitioned into his new career, my mom continued running her in-home daycare. When Eric was adopted, my mom and older sister, Brooke, traveled to Thailand to bring him home. I stayed behind with my dad and Grandma Coleman when he had to work. I only remember pieces of that time without my mom.

One memory stands out vividly: one evening, I crept into her room and grabbed a shirt she often wore. It was striped with shades of brown, the kind she paired with jeans for everyday wear or nicer pants for church. The shirt wasn't hard to find, but it still carried her scent, her signature designer perfume. I smuggled it back to my room, tucked it beneath my pillow, and slept with it for comfort, hiding it away during the day. That shirt was my tether to her.

To ease my separation anxiety, my mom had prepared small gift bags for each day she was away. Each bag contained a note and a small toy. Every morning, I looked forward to discovering what she had left for me. Toward the end of her trip, I opened one to find a Barbie film camera. The note said I could take photos and that she would bring photos back from her travels so we could compare. I guarded that camera carefully, waiting for Eric's arrival so I could capture it.

When the day came, my dad and I went to the airport. Just as before, family and friends gathered in anticipation. Watching the excitement around me, I wondered if my own arrival had felt the same way. Clutching my Barbie camera, I felt both nervous and excited, determined to document everything.

At last, people began filing through the gate. My dad's eyes were fixed on the crowd, scanning eagerly. And then, there they were: my mom, Brooke, and my new not-so-baby brother. I quickly raised my camera, looked through the tiny viewfinder, and clicked. A small flash confirmed it: my very first photograph.

I got into a rhythm, clicking again and again, desperate to capture every moment. As everyone gathered around Eric, I proudly kept photographing. Until, suddenly, the button wouldn't press. Alarmed, I handed it to my mom. She smiled and explained that the camera wasn't broken; it was out of film. "We'll need to have it developed," she said. I didn't know what that meant, but I trusted her.

Later, we took the film to the store. A man behind the counter collected the tiny roll while we wandered the aisles, waiting impatiently. Finally, the photos were ready. My heart pounded with pride, knowing I had captured such an important memory.

But when my mom opened the envelope, her face shifted. At first, she looked puzzled. My heart sank; I thought I'd done something wrong. Then, suddenly, she burst out laughing. I pulled out my Barbie photo album, ready to carefully place each photo inside its slot. She handed them to me one by one, her laughter growing louder as I examined them.

Every single picture was either of people's belly buttons or the ground. A few included Eric, but they were blurry, the result of my impatience or his movement. My "masterpiece" turned out to be a comic disaster.

It became clear: photography was not going to be my calling. I happily left that art form to my older sister Brooke, whose creative abilities flourished beautifully. Looking back now, I realize that those belly-button photographs said more about me than I knew; they revealed a child eager to participate, desperate to contribute, but not yet able to capture the world the way I imagined it.

The house now held my parents, my older sister Brooke, myself, and my new little brother, Eric. My two older siblings, Geoff and Natalie, were either living with their dad or on their own, since they were much older.

Living with a little brother was… tolerable at best. He never listened, always played with toys "the wrong" way, and had the disturbing habit of putting everything into his mouth, including, but not limited to, parts of his own body. "Gross," I would declare with unfiltered disgust, my face making it clear I meant it. He never cared, of course, and carried on as though my protests didn't exist.

Looking back, I realize I resented him at first. My parents hadn't needed to go out of their way to adopt another sibling who looked like me, or anyone at all. I had loved being the baby of the family. Now, I wasn't. The pure audacity!

But as I sulked in my self-pity, Eric began to grow on me. Against my will, I started taking on what I thought were "big sister responsibilities." Still, I wasn't exactly selfless. Instead of simply teaching him what not to do, I often modeled the "wrong" behavior and then blamed him for copying me. It worked… until the day it didn't. At the time, though, it felt like delicious revenge.

A year later, it was time for me to start elementary school. I enrolled at Crestland Elementary, located in downtown Kansas, for the 2001–2002 school year. My mom was hesitant at first. She worried I might struggle to adapt in a public-school setting. My dad, however, encouraged my excitement. He believed being in school would be good for me, helping me grow socially and giving me experiences beyond the walls of home. My mom reluctantly agreed, promising that if I didn't like it, I could always be homeschooled.

I don't remember much from kindergarten, but certain moments stuck and later revealed themselves as foundational memories. At the time, though, I was simply thrilled. There's a picture of me from my first day of school: I wore a red Raggedy Ann dress handmade by my mom, a white T-shirt underneath, and my hair pulled into pigtails tied with red ribbons. My socks had little ruffles, and on my back was a navy-blue Winnie the Pooh and Tigger backpack. I was in heaven.

But what began as heaven quickly descended into something closer to hell. At age five, I didn't yet understand the word "hell," but I knew I wasn't in a safe or comfortable place.

Most of my kindergarten memories are punctuated by time spent in the principal's office. I was not the best-behaved student, and my grades reflected my struggles. I remember my teacher placing stickers at the top of my notebook pages, reminding me to stay inside the designated lines for coloring. I remember assignments coming home marked with giant capital letters: "C" or "D."

Even now, thinking back stings. It stings even more as a mother myself, knowing one of my own children has already gone through kindergarten. I didn't fit in, not just because of shyness, but because I was different. I had one or two friends, but only one true best friend, a boy named Beck. And I remember, with equal clarity, the classmates who openly mocked me.

At home, I was loved, accepted, and celebrated. Out in the world, I discovered for the first time that others didn't always see me the same way. I hadn't realized I was different until I was surrounded by children who made it their mission to point it out.

Other parents even told my mom they thought my teacher was unfairly biased against me. My mom and dad saw it too, but they decided not to make a scene and allowed me to finish out the year. When I acted out, the punishment was always the same: I was sent to sit at a lone desk in the back of the classroom, right beside the cubbies and the shared bathroom. That isolation cut deeper than any lecture could. Sitting alone like that only highlighted my differences, giving the other kids even more ammunition.

Three classmates, in particular, made it their daily ritual to remind me that I didn't belong. I can still hear their voices teasing me about my "Walmart shoes," or what they assumed were Walmart shoes. And, truthfully, they were right; my shoes weren't Nike or Adidas. But children grow so fast, and shoes wear down so quickly. Now, as a parent myself, I completely understand why my mom chose practicality over labels. At the time, though, the ridicule burned.

Their cruelty escalated: "Your parents had to pay too much money to buy you," they would sneer, "so they couldn't afford nice shoes." They laughed, pointing proudly to the brands stamped on their own sneakers.

It's strange, the way those words lodge in your memory, as sharp decades later as they were in the moment.

I also remember playtime at the classroom "stations." Sometimes we rotated into a neighboring classroom where different sections were set up: a block station, an art corner, and a play kitchen. A timer ensured everyone got a turn. One afternoon, it was my group's turn in the kitchen.

The kitchens back then were flimsy, plastic sets, nothing like the realistic replicas kids play with today. In my group were the three girls who tormented me daily and, thankfully, my best friend, Beck. One of the "mean girls," the tallest of the bunch, took charge immediately. She assigned roles: she was the mom, Beck was the dad, and the other two girls were her daughters.

That left me.

I stood there, holding my breath, hoping, just hoping, they would assign me something harmless. In my mind, I thought maybe I could be an aunt, or perhaps just another daughter. Anything that let me belong.

Then the words came, quick and sharp, slicing into me before I could even prepare for them.

She looked at me, pretending to think hard about what role to assign. Finally, she smirked and said, *"And for you... you can be the dog or the maid."*

Confusion washed over me, quickly replaced by disappointment. "Why do I have to be an animal or a maid?" I asked, my voice small but determined.

Her answer was matter-of-fact, as though it were the most logical thing in the world. *"Because that's the only thing that makes sense."*

Desperate to belong, I pushed back. "Can I just be another daughter?" I pleaded, hoping she would reconsider.

But what came next broke something inside me. "No. You can't be a daughter. I already have two, and you're not the same color as them or me."

The words pierced me before I could even process them. My chest tightened, and my eyes burned. Before I knew it, tears were spilling down my cheeks.

The moment they saw me cry, laughter erupted. *"Look at the baby crying,"* she taunted, her voice sharp and merciless. As if that weren't enough, she added, *"If you want to play with us, you have to be the dog."*

Anger bubbled up inside me. "I'm not a dog!" I shouted back, my voice shaking.

But she only smirked, leaning in closer to twist the knife. *"Get on the floor like a dog. Bark like a dog."*

Her mockery dripped with cruelty. And though I tried to stand my ground, the attention our back-and-forth drew only made things worse. The teacher walked over, assessing the situation.

Of course, the girl spun the story to her advantage: "We're just playing house, but Autumn doesn't want to play nice."

My teacher scanned the group, her face expressionless. Every child stared back at her, waiting to see how she'd respond. Then her eyes landed on me. She scratched at her neck, her nervous habit, leaving red marks across her skin as she thought. I held my breath, praying she would defend me, allow me a chance to play the role I wanted, or at least acknowledge the unfairness of what had just happened.

But instead, she sighed. "Autumn, go sit down at the table. If you can't get along, then you'll have to sit out."

The weight of her words sank into me like cement. My head dropped as I walked to the table. Behind me, I heard the sting of one final comment: *"She wouldn't be a good dog anyway, she's bad."*

My heart plummeted into my stomach. I sat in a cold chair, alone, watching as the other children continued to laugh and play until station time ended.

After that day, my mom had to bribe me with Burger King Cinna-Minis just to coax me out of the car each morning at drop-off. Those small sugary spirals became my only incentive to face a place where difference meant rejection.

Looking back, I can see it clearly: it was in moments like those that I first learned what it meant to be *different*.

There's a photo that captures this truth more starkly than words ever could. It was taken on a field trip to the aquarium. In the photo, my teacher sits proudly in the center, surrounded by her smiling students. And where am I? Off to the far right, seated next to the one child who tolerated me. Decades later, that very same "mean girl" posted the photo online as a "throwback." Until then, I had forgotten it even existed. But seeing it again was like reopening an old wound.

Then came September 11, 2001. A day that shook not just the country, but the very sense of safety in my five-year-old world.

That morning began like any other in kindergarten. We settled into our seats as the teacher outlined the day's activities. Suddenly, the classroom phone rang. She walked over to answer it, and as she listened, her expression changed. What began as mild curiosity transformed into something heavier: confusion, then concern.

Even as children, we could feel it. The air in the room shifted, weighted with something we couldn't name. We all grew quiet, watching her closely, waiting.

A few minutes later, the intercom crackled to life. A voice, heavy with urgency, announced that parents would be coming to pick up their children. If our names were called, we were to gather our belongings and head to the office. None of us knew what was happening, but the teachers and staff did their best to remain calm, shielding us from their own alarm. Still, I noticed my teacher's eyes glisten with unshed tears as she tried to hold it together.

At first, I wasn't scared. To me, being picked up early sounded like a gift. Any reason to leave school felt like a good one. So, when my name was called, I hurried to pack my things, buzzing with excitement.

But that excitement died the instant I saw my mom waiting for me. Her eyes were swollen, her cheeks red from crying. Something was wrong, something bigger than I could grasp. My chest grew heavy, and I felt sadness creep in, though I didn't yet understand why. Looking around, I noticed every adult's face carried the same weight: tear-stained, solemn, broken.

We drove home in silence. I don't remember the specifics of that afternoon, but I'll never forget the image of sitting on the family room floor, the TV glowing in front of me. My parents sat on the couch, my mom sobbing into her hands. On the screen, smoke billowed, people screamed, and anchors spoke words too fast for me to fully comprehend.

I turned to my parents, wide-eyed. "What's happening?" I asked.

They exchanged a glance as though they'd forgotten I was even there. Then they looked at me with deliberate care. They explained that very bad men had taken over airplanes filled with people and crashed them into two important buildings in a city called New York.

I turned back to the TV, trying to picture their words, trying to make sense of it all. The room was silent except for the haunting noise of the broadcast. My eyes blurred with tears as the realization settled in, even in my child's mind: so many people had died.

For days, weeks, and even months afterward, 9/11 consumed everything. The TV played the footage on repeat. Radios carried the same news. Magazines, newspapers, and grocery store racks, all filled with the same images of smoke, rubble, and grief. Everywhere I went, it seemed like people were crying, or had been crying for a very long time.

Flags appeared on nearly every house along our street and the neighboring ones. If you hadn't owned an American flag before, you certainly had one now. Patriotism wasn't just encouraged, it was expected.

Years later, my high school history teacher told us something that stayed with me: anyone who was at least five years old in 2001 is among the youngest and last people who truly *remember* the attacks of 9/11. That struck me. To carry a memory so collective, yet so heavy, is both a burden and a responsibility.

In the wake of tragedy, the country seemed to breathe as one. Families clung to each other tightly. Neighbors checked in on neighbors. Strangers showed unexpected kindness. It was as though the United States had suddenly become a single, grieving household. Yet alongside the unity came something else, an undercurrent of fear, sadness, and anger that froze everything in place. People were afraid to fly. Life felt suspended, as though the world itself had been knocked off its axis.

I was still very young, too young to grasp the full weight of what had happened. I couldn't understand why my parents cried over strangers, why grief poured out of people for faces they'd never known. But I noticed how the conversations always circled back to the attacks. Every dinner table, every grocery store checkout line, every overheard exchange, it all returned to 9/11.

And in those conversations, I noticed a shift. Alongside compassion, fear and anger began to creep in. People wanted justice and needed it. They wanted action, retribution, something to make sense of the senseless. Their words, raw and unfiltered, spilled out, and others nodded along, echoing their pain. These emotions were valid, even natural, but for me, the fallout was different.

Life, already difficult, became almost unbearable. Suddenly, I was picked on more and more for the color of my skin. Children, too young to truly understand, repeated words they had absorbed from their parents like parrots, words sharp enough to cut. At times, it felt like they blamed me personally, as though *I* had been the one to board those planes and steer them into buildings.

When kindergarten ended, I made up my mind: I didn't want to go back. I hated the feeling of being left out, of being mocked, of being made to feel responsible for something I couldn't even comprehend.

My sadness was layered with a determination to protect myself. But protection soon gave way to something darker.

For years, I let the hurt fester. I resented those children. I hated them. That anger, unchecked, sat heavy inside me and hardened with time. It wasn't until high school, maybe even later, as a young adult, that I finally began to loosen my grip on the pain I had carried for so long.

I no longer hold resentment toward the children who mocked me, or the classmates who laughed at my expense. For a while, I told myself I was simply too serious, that I lacked a sense of humor. I even tried to take the blame, convincing myself their cruelty was somehow my fault. But in truth, children are mirrors. At five years old, they don't yet have the wisdom to filter what they hear. They reflect their parents, their guardians, and their environment. Their minds are sponges, soaking up every word, every attitude, and every offhand comment dropped within earshot.

Now, as an adult, I can see it differently. I imagine those same children going home and asking their parents, *"Why is Autumn a different color than her mom and dad?"* And maybe the answers weren't gentle. Maybe the words weren't even directed at the child, but the child still heard them and still absorbed them. Those careless words, spoken in kitchens or living rooms, came tumbling out later in classrooms and playgrounds, hurled at me like stones.

I could place the blame on their parents. Perhaps I should. But carrying that kind of weight has never been my nature. I've always leaned toward empathy, toward giving people the benefit of the doubt. Back then, adoption was still a foreign concept to many. And when people don't understand something, they often turn to jokes, to mockery, to whatever makes the discomfort easier to bear. It doesn't excuse their words, but it explains them. Most cruelty, I've come to realize, is born of fear, not malice.

Still, for me, the damage had already been done. The U.S. and China weren't on the best of terms in the early 2000s, and the terrorist attacks only deepened suspicions and divisions. I carried hatred in my heart for those children, hatred so sharp that I could still name each of them, even today. But naming them isn't my purpose here. What matters is what became of me because of that hatred.

The bullied, over time, became the bully. My pain didn't just sit inside me; it spilled out, often in the unkindest of ways.

Chapter 4:
A Homeschooled Traveler

After kindergarten, I was officially homeschooled by my mom. Our curriculum came from the schoolbooks sold at a popular Christian bookstore. At the back of the store, there was a section dedicated to classrooms and learning. Each grade had its own area, covering every subject while aligning with Christian values and meeting the required educational standards. It was comparable to the public school system, even before families were required to regularly submit work to the state.

It felt as though we lived in an invisible bubble, safe from the world and unnoticed in our existence. My brother and I once visited a local Christian academy during a school day to observe their daily operations firsthand. This helped my mom gain a sense of what she needed to teach us and the environment she wanted to create. She did her best to model our home classroom after theirs.

We woke up each morning, dressed in uniforms, ate breakfast, and sat at our desks. Our classroom was my old bedroom. To create a functional learning space, my parents moved me upstairs to a room with Eric. We even got bunk beds, the sturdy metal kind that became popular in the early 2000s. I had the top bunk, and Eric had the bottom, only because I was older and could handle the ladder better. The bunk bed seemed practical and exciting for a while, but soon enough, I grew to hate that piece of furniture. When my brother was angry or irritated, he would shove his feet between the bars and kick my mattress with his heels, delivering heavy kicks in a fast and repetitive manner, just to annoy me.

In my old room, my mom put in a desk with attached seats secured by metal bars connected to the writing surface, and the tops opened up to store our books and supplies. Along one wall sat two shelves filled with school materials and activities. My mom's large metal and plastic table held her computer. This was the start of my real learning journey, free from the bullying and strict rules of public school.

I was excited to learn, excited to be at home, and especially excited to work at my own pace. It even meant I could sometimes finish my school day earlier than my older siblings. I loved the structure, the uniforms, and the rhythm of our small classroom. Eric, however, ended up being held back a year. Having just been adopted from Thailand, he was still learning English, and schoolwork was difficult for him. All my mom's focus in those early years fell on me as the first grader. I envied him at times, especially when I saw him lounging on the couch, watching TV for most of the day while I was hard at work. My mom would call him over occasionally to practice English, but if he grew restless or fussy, she quickly sent him off to play. With me, she was far stricter.

Homeschooling became my world, and it would remain that way for the rest of my education.

During those early years, my mom was heavily involved in adoption groups through email. One member mentioned the "Foreign Exchange Student Program" as an opportunity for families to host students from the same countries their children came from. My mom thought it might help Eric adjust if someone from Thailand lived with us. She also thought it might be beneficial for me. That's how we met Daisy.

Daisy came from Bangkok and stayed with us for two years while attending high school with my older sister. She was kind, patient, and full of stories about Thailand. I thought of her as another older sister during the time she lived with us. When her two years ended, she returned to Thailand to finish high school and continue her life. At the time, I didn't know I would cross paths with her again in the future.

Though my parents had always been open about the fact that I was adopted, and though I met people such as Daisy, I still did not fully understand what it meant to be an adopted child. I was seven years old the day it truly hit me; I came to the realization that I was not born to my mom and dad. Before that, I believed I had come from them. The differences others pointed out at school or in public didn't connect in my mind. There were baby pictures to prove I was once a baby in their arms, and in my young mind, that was enough.

I remember sitting at a restaurant with my older sister. We wore matching outfits that day: blue jeans, white T-shirts, and baby blue button-up sweaters. My mom looked across the booth at us and said, "Wow, you both look so alike." Without hesitation, I replied firmly, "We do not look alike." They stared at me, waiting for the obvious. Instead, I said, "She has pimples, and I don't."

My mom laughed, and my sister giggled, though she was understandably a little upset. But she knew, as she always did, that I hadn't meant to be cruel. The truth was, I didn't yet see the real difference between us. I didn't grasp it…not then.

One Sunday, either on the way to church or coming home from it, I noticed a car near us with a bumper sticker that read: *Abortion stops a beating heart.* I was just learning to read and sounded it out aloud. "What does that mean?" I asked my mom.

She paused, caught off guard by my out-of-the-blue question. As the car with the sticker pulled ahead, she realized where it came from. Keeping her eyes on the road, she explained gently. "That means being pro-life. It means a woman chooses to have her baby, no matter the circumstances."

My brows furrowed.

"Like your mom," she added after a moment.

"My mom?" I asked.

"Yes," she said, "your birth mom, not me."

I nodded, but confusion still clouded my thoughts. It was the first time I began to sense that my story carried layers I didn't yet fully understand.

She continued speaking with conviction and a motherly instinct. She told me that my birth mother in China chose to have me instead of letting me die in her tummy. She chose to give me life instead of death.

I remember sitting in my car seat, right behind the driver's seat, when her words sank in. A wave of emotions crashed over me, and I began to cry in loud, uncontrollable sobs. In that moment, every puzzle piece in my mind seemed to click into place, revealing a picture I hadn't been ready to see.

As my mom continued, she explained that I had not grown in her tummy, which was why I looked different from my older siblings. Even Eric, who resembled me more than they did, still looked different. She used Eric's adoption as another example, reminding me that neither of us was biologically related to her. My heart beat faster as I stared out the window, feeling happy and sad at the same time.

I was happy that my birth mother had chosen to give me life; otherwise, I wouldn't exist. But sadness followed quickly. I had so many questions: Why hadn't she wanted me? Why had she given me up? Was I not what she expected? Did she dislike me? Was she disappointed?

The questions ran wild in my mind, but I wasn't ready to voice them. The feeling of not being wanted lingered faintly inside me. It was an emotion I would avoid facing directly for many years to come. The car ride ended in silence, but my thoughts didn't quiet down. Through all the confusion, one thing was certain: I felt different.

As time passed, our homeschooling continued. Each year brought a new set of books suited to our grade level. Our social life mainly came from church and the homeschool groups my mom joined. We often went on field trips with other homeschooling children, turning nearly every outing into a chance to learn.

One of the most memorable was to Aldi's grocery store. My brother and I each carried calculators. We were tasked with adding up the cost of the groceries, including tax, and whoever got closest to the final amount would win a prize. The prize, most of the time, was lunch at McDonald's. Looking back as a parent, I laugh at how the "special prize" was food we needed anyway, and at a fast-food restaurant with the creepiest clown. To this day, you cannot convince me that clowns are funny or cute.

My brother and I were fiercely competitive, so every contest turned into an argument about who really won. And if I'm honest (and this is something I'll only admit here), I often cheated. At Aldi's, I positioned myself so I could see the cashier's monitor as items were scanned. While Eric focused on the customer-facing screen, I adjusted my calculator to match the total. Those old calculators didn't display the steps taken to reach the answer, so naturally, I "won" most of the time. Either way, we usually ended up at McDonald's.

Since our curriculum was expensive, my mom continued her in-home daycare for children who hadn't started school yet. However, as those children grew old enough for public school, their numbers declined, and no new children replaced them.

Eventually, my mom began watching our neighbor's little boy. He came over in the mornings and stayed until evening pickup, right after our nap time. When he was old enough to start preschool, he attended in the mornings. We would pick him up afterward and watch him for the rest of the day. While he was at preschool, we focused on schoolwork. If we hadn't finished by the time we picked him up and had lunch, we returned to it later in the day. Once we were done, we played with him until his parents arrived. We had a steady routine, and as the years passed, life on Hadley Street in Merriam, Kansas, seemed to move smoothly.

Not long after kindergarten ended, my mom leaned deeper into her passion for adoption. Having adopted two children herself, she became an adoption agent while balancing her many other roles. She met many people through this work, and one of them was Michelle, who would become a dear friend not just to her but to me as well.

It was 2003 when I was given the opportunity to travel with my mom and Michelle to help eleven families adopt their babies from China. All the parents chipped in for my flight, believing that, because I was adopted, my presence might ease the transition for their children. I was thrilled. The idea of flying on a plane, especially to another country, filled me with excitement. The first thought that came to my mind was, *You wouldn't get to do this if you were in public school.*

As we prepared for the flight overseas, I was eager and curious, unaware of what lay ahead or what I was about to experience.

Our first stop was Bangkok, Thailand, where we stayed for about a week in Daisy's parents' home. Daisy had been our foreign exchange student, and her parents graciously opened their doors to us in return for what my mom had done for her. Their home was lovely, and our time in Thailand was unforgettable.

Bangkok surprised me, it was hotter, more humid, and dustier than I had imagined. If you showered and stepped outside right after, the roads kicked up so much dust that you were instantly covered again. During that week, I tried congee for the first time. I had never tasted anything like it, and to this day, it remains one of my favorite Thai dishes.

I also remember my mom's warnings every time we took a bath. "Keep your eyes and mouth shut," she reminded me, since Thailand's water wasn't purified and we weren't staying in a hotel. She even told me to brush my teeth with bottled water. The thought of unseen parasites lurking in the water left me both cautious and fascinated.

Standing there brushing my teeth, I suddenly remembered the time when Eric first came home. My dad had taken him upstairs to change his diaper. Then came a scream, not of fear, but of deep concern.

"Trish!!?" His voice echoed through the house.

"Yes?" my mom answered.

"You need to come see this," he called back.

My mom could tell that something was wrong, so she rushed upstairs, skipping steps in her urgency. I ran after her, nosy as ever.

My dad was kneeling on the floor, waiting anxiously for her arrival. Eric was propped up in front of him. As soon as my mom entered the room, she looked at Eric. Realizing he was okay, she looked confused and asked, "What?"

I squeezed past her, positioning myself between them, eager to see the cause of all the fuss.

My dad rarely yelled across the house. He hated it. The only times he raised his voice were when he wanted Eric or me to bring him coffee or when he needed to get my mom's attention while doing something he probably shouldn't have been doing. So, when he shouted, it meant something unusual had happened.

As he pulled back the front of Eric's diaper, my mom gasped in shock. My eyes widened like pennies. I tried to stay silent as I processed what I saw. Inside the diaper squirmed a thin white creature, as long as a pencil, writhing and alive.

"Well, we'd better set an appointment with the doctor," my mom said quickly.

My dad nodded quickly, his hands slightly shaking. (After that, I don't think my dad ever changed a diaper again.)

I stared at the disgusting, odd-looking thing and finally blurted, "What is that?"

"It's a tapeworm," my mom replied.

"What's a tapeworm?" I asked.

Still focused on the diaper, she explained, "It's a worm in the drinking water in Thailand. It starts out small, and then it grows to this size. Eventually, they come out."

I stood there, baffled. How could something from inside Eric end up crawling into his diaper? Within minutes, the realization hit me. "Ohhhhh. Oh no. Oh gross."

My dad turned fifty shades of green at what he was witnessing. Eric, meanwhile, lay there calmly, waiting to be changed, as if this were nothing new.

I shook my head, covering my mouth dramatically, convinced I might throw up. If Eric hadn't already been "gross" in my mind simply for being a boy, he had officially earned the title. But I have to give him credit; he was only three, far too little to understand or control what was happening.

I snapped back to the present, realizing I was still brushing my teeth. Panic crept in. *What if water got in my mouth while I was distracted? What if I had a parasite growing inside me?* My imagination spiraled until I nearly gave myself a panic attack picturing a worm crawling out of me while I slept.

While in Thailand, we also toured the world-renowned Floating Market. As my mom and Michelle browsed the stalls, I wandered, taking in the sights. My gaze drifted toward the Chao Phraya River, and I froze.

There, in the water, a man was bathing. He scrubbed his armpits and face, working up a lather. A pool of bubbles surrounded him. I couldn't believe my eyes. It was a person taking a bath in what looked, to me, like a giant swimming pool. My seven-year-old brain didn't yet grasp the concept of rivers.

Later, I would learn that the Chao Phraya River is one of Thailand's major rivers, with a wide alluvial plain that forms the country's center. It flows through Bangkok and into the Gulf of Thailand. But at that moment, I simply stared and chose not to say a word to anyone.

Soon after, my mom and Michelle decided to take a banana boat across the wide river. Along the way, we saw countless shoes floating by. My mom and Michelle laughed at the sight. I looked at them, puzzled. My mom, noticing my expression, explained that they found it funny the same way they laughed at seeing random shoes in the U.S. thrown on the side of a road or hanging from a power line. I didn't understand, but I laughed too, eager to be part of their moment.

As we drifted further, we passed something breathtaking: the King's Golden Boat, gleaming inside its water garage. Whenever the King traveled, he rode this massive vessel made of pure gold. I couldn't take my eyes off it.

Thailand offered other wonders, too. One that caught my heart was *Hello Kitty*. At that time, the character hadn't yet reached the U.S., but in Thailand, it was everywhere. I became instantly obsessed. I wore a thin blue nightgown with ruffles along the collar, patterned with tiny *Hello Kitty* faces outlined in dark blue. I even got a *Hello Kitty* fork and spoon set, metal at the head, with pink handles stamped with the name. At the top of each handle was *Hello Kitty's* smiling face.

Before leaving Thailand, we went to a dinner show. The setup looked like a theater, but instead of rows of chairs, there were long black booths. From the front, you couldn't see anyone behind you. The performance was entirely in Thai, strange and fascinating to us.

Michelle also decided to get a haircut while we were there. At the salon, instead of being led to a sink, she sat in the chair as the stylist poured water from a Sprite bottle onto her head. There was no running water. The shop was primitive, and soon a crowd of women gathered to watch. They were fascinated. Michelle's hair was pure blonde, a rarity that drew every eye.

I loved my time in Thailand, but soon enough, it was time to head to Kunming, China, where we would meet all eleven families adopting their babies. We spent two weeks in China, split between Kunming and Guangzhou. While in Kunming, we visited a local orphanage.

One day, my mom was busy helping the other mothers, and I stood in the hallway, quietly waiting. Behind me was a window. I turned and peered through it into a small courtyard where children were playing in a worn playground. They belonged to the orphanage. As I watched them, tears welled in my eyes and spilled down my cheeks. One of the mothers noticed and went to tell my mom. She hurried out and joined me at the window.

She followed my gaze to the children outside. When she turned back to me, I saw it in her eyes: understanding, empathy, and almost a glisten of remorse for what she knew I was feeling. At that moment, I could no longer hide from the truth: I had come from an orphanage. The scene outside that glassless window had once been my reality.

This was not the first time the realization hit me, nor would it be the last. Throughout my young life, moments like these would strike suddenly like lights flicked on in a dark room, reminding me of where I had come from. However, as time passed and I gained a better understanding of my situation, it became easier to cope with the intense emotions. After all, there were some truly beautiful aspects of adoption.

When the time came for the parents to meet their babies, I stood in awe. One by one, each mother received her child with tears streaming down her face. I tried to imagine what it must have been like for my own mother when she first received me. A warmth spread through me. I closed my eyes and smiled, picturing that moment, almost as if I could travel back in time and experience it myself.

But as I stood there, I also thought about the birth mothers. Tears pricked my eyes again as I realized each of these babies had been let go by a woman who must have carried the same ache as my own birth mother. The sacrifice they made was heavy, yet it gave their children a chance at a life they themselves could not provide. That knowledge gave me both sorrow and peace. It was a bittersweet truth, an immeasurable loss traded for a priceless gift.

After all the parents had received their babies, we traveled to Guangzhou. We stayed at the White Swan Hotel, just as we had six years earlier. Only this time, I remembered it clearly. As each family checked in, the front desk handed them a token box. When I saw the smiles on the parents' faces, I asked to see one. They handed me the plastic case, and inside was a Barbie doll holding a tiny baby with black hair.

I stared at it and saw myself in that little doll. My mom noticed my expression and gently reminded me that I had one just like it at home, carefully tucked away as a keepsake.

I think this little black-haired doll was why I loved Barbies so much growing up. Barbies had always been the highlight of my childhood. I remembered my first Barbie, a gift when I was six, that came with a pink sports car complete with little white plastic seatbelts that actually clicked into place. My favorite, though, was my 1998 Barbie Family Victorian Folding Cottage. It was blue, and when you opened it, it revealed a cozy interior with a sitting area, a kitchen, and a fold-down bed. Even the phone rang. It came with tiny pink plates and silverware, and it quickly became the centerpiece of my play.

I even played Barbies with my dad. One of my fondest memories was playing the "Dating Game" with him. He used his deep announcer voice, pretending Barbie was the contestant behind the house and the Kens were the bachelors. He lay on his side on the carpet, legs folded, propping his head on his hand while picking up each Ken to answer my questions. I would giggle at how seriously he played the role. These games with my dad left lasting memories, moments that reminded me I was chosen, loved, and wanted.

The little Barbie that the parents had shown me reminded me of these warm feelings. Smiling, I handed it back to the child, telling them it was very special. They took it with stars in their eyes, clutching it as if it were the first thing that had ever been truly theirs.

Later, we explored the nearby marketplace. While my mom browsed the tightly packed shops, I stood quietly, taking it all in. Suddenly, a small Chinese woman approached me and said something I didn't understand. Reflexively, I responded, "I don't understand you. I speak English."

She blinked in surprise, then smiled. "Oh, you speak English?"

My mom quickly came up beside me. The woman explained, "Would you care to speak with my students from the university?" My mom nodded in agreement, and we followed her.

She led us into a smoke-filled tobacco shop, where she lifted me onto a giant bale of tobacco. From that vantage point, I could see the entire shop. Ten Chinese men gathered around me, notebooks in hand. I began speaking, and they repeated after me. If they didn't catch it, I repeated myself until they did. The woman mouthed the words with them, nodding encouragement. They wrote everything down carefully, practicing again and again until they got it right.

In that moment, I felt important. I felt like I mattered. I wasn't just a child tagging along; I was someone who could help. When we finally left the shop, each of them bowed to me out of respect.

For once, in a place where I often felt I didn't belong, I had found a moment of belonging.

Back at the hotel, my mom received a call from another family needing her help. She asked Michelle to watch me, promising she'd be back soon. Michelle agreed, and my mom quickly left the room.

I was sitting on the bed, busy with one of the little activities my mom had packed to keep me entertained. After a while, I looked up and asked Michelle if I could take a bath. She smiled and said yes, then went into the bathroom to prepare it.

The hotel provided tiny bottles of bubble bath, so she emptied one into the tub and started the water. I jumped in eagerly and watched the bubbles rise, fascinated by how they feathered and floated in my hands.

Michelle stepped away for barely a minute, but when she returned, the bubbles were spilling over the edge of the tub, towering far above the bathtub walls. She gasped, rushed to turn off the water, and called out, "Autumn?"

I parted the bubbles, poked my head out, and looked at her with foam clinging to my cheeks. She laughed, amazed at how quickly the bubbles had multiplied. Settling beside me, she opened her book while I lost myself in play, pretending I was inside a house built of bubbles. I leaned back, gazing up at my towering bubble walls, completely hidden from the outside world. Michelle didn't worry, though. She could still hear the swish of water every time I shifted.

Suddenly, we heard a buzz. It was the hotel door. Someone was swiping a key card. The door opened, and my mom stepped inside. She followed the light straight to the bathroom and stopped short, eyes wide. "Wow!" she exclaimed.

Michelle looked up and agreed, smiling. I peeked through the bubbles again, foam-covered face grinning, and my mom laughed. "These are some bubbles, all right."

At home, she would have to pour nearly an entire bottle, 12 or even 20 ounces, just to get a thin layer of foam, and even then, it would fade quickly. These bubbles were stubborn and magical, lasting for hours even after the tub had been drained. By the time I got out, my fingers were so wrinkled they looked like shriveled-up French fries. From that day on, Michelle nicknamed me "Bubble Girl."

As our trip continued, we explored the streets daily. Everywhere we went, people stared. My mom and Michelle were two of the palest people most locals had ever seen, and I stood out too, as I was dressed neatly, almost too primly. It made the people think that I came from great wealth. Their gazes followed us, sometimes with such intensity that it caused accidents. I still remember one woman on a bicycle who crashed straight into a car pulling out of an alley because she couldn't stop staring. Another woman walked directly into a tree. I didn't know whether to feel embarrassed or important.

The streets were alive with the noise of markets. Vendors called out, shouting numbers at us like auctioneers, each trying to outdo the other with lower prices, as if we were the prize to be won.

The food was delicious, but I missed the comforts of home. When we finally spotted a McDonald's, my heart leapt. I hadn't eaten one in weeks, and the thought of a cheeseburger made me almost giddy.

But as soon as we stepped inside, I realized this McDonald's wasn't like home. To the left was a small playground with a slide that dropped kids off right by the door. The menu above the counter was filled with pictures paired with Chinese characters. I was skeptical, but I decided to trust the food.

My mom ordered for us, and when the food arrived, I took a huge bite of my burger.

Instant regret.

"Ugh, pickles and mustard—yuck!" I sputtered, spitting the bite back out. I looked at my mom, wide-eyed, wondering if she realized what I'd just tasted. She knew I always ordered cheeseburgers with ketchup only. Surely, being in another country hadn't made her forget that.

She took one look at me and said, "This is different, Autumn."

I froze, my face full of concern and confusion.

"This is China, and McDonald's has to follow specific rules here. They are not allowed to serve you food unless it looks exactly like the picture." She pointed to one of the menus with a picture of a cheeseburger.

I turned slowly toward the bright candescent menu board glowing above the counter, studying the photos with new eyes. Did they really expect us to know what each burger contained just by the picture? I squinted at it, then looked back at my mom, silently asking what I was supposed to do. Surely, I couldn't starve to death over a cheeseburger.

She gave me that ridiculous look she always wore when she thought I was being dramatic. Meanwhile, I still had the sour taste of mustard and pickles in my mouth.

"Just scrape off what you don't want," she said flatly.

I stared at her, thinking, *does she not understand how impossible that is? If you scrape it off, you lose the ketchup too!* Of course, I didn't dare say that out loud if I wanted to survive. So, with a disappointed sigh and a disgusted look, I scraped the toppings off. What sat in front of me looked like the saddest burger I had ever seen. Still, I ate it.

Then it was toy time. I always looked forward to McDonald's toys because every visit usually meant a new piece of the collection. Kids went in with the dream of collecting the full set. If you ended up with a duplicate, you could even ask the worker to swap it with a different toy from the bin.

Did I expect the toy here in China to bring me the same joy? Absolutely not. Instead of fun collectibles, the toys were educational. Mine was a set of tiny, brightly colored ovals that, when fitted together correctly, formed a ball.

A math problem. That's what they gave me. A toy math problem.

I sat there, fumbling with the pieces, growing increasingly frustrated by the second. Michelle eventually took the toy from me and, with surprising ease, pieced it together using the printed instructions (written in Chinese, of course). She must have followed the shaded diagrams that represented the neon colors. I'll never understand how that worked.

When she finally handed the toy back, it collapsed the second I touched it. My face fell, disappointment and irritation written all over me.

My mom picked up the pieces, promising, "When we get back to the hotel, I'll tape it so it won't come apart."

Looking back now, I realize how many little concessions she made for me on that trip. As a mom myself, I probably wouldn't have done half of what she did. Honestly, I was spoiled.

Our trip eventually came to an end, and we boarded the plane for the return home. At the time, I thought this would be my last trip overseas for years, never imagining I'd return one day. My mom, however, would make another trip abroad without me, this time with other adults and no children. Naturally, planning was far easier that way.

When we got back, Eric did not speak to us for a while. He was upset that I got to go on the trip and even more upset that he had been left behind. I did feel a little bad for him. But at the same time, I finally had the rare privilege of being the oldest sibling. And in my mind, that meant I had earned the right to go.

Chapter 5:
Through Grandma's Door

In 2004, when I was 8 years old, my family faced one of our great losses. The death of a loved one for the first time. My Grandma Coleman passed away in July of 2004. She had been sick for a few months and was cared for by the nurses who came to the house, along with their children, my aunts, and my mom. I remember spending hours over there in the living room while my mom tended to her needs. I also saw more of my dad's side of the family during that time. My aunts, uncles, and cousins would fly in to spend as much time as possible with Grandma before she passed.

After my grandma died that December, my parents decided to buy my grandparents' house from the siblings to keep it in the family. The house had been built in 1964 when my dad was just three years old.

I never knew my Grandpa Coleman, as he passed before I was adopted. Another person I never met was my dad's older brother, who died in his twenties. My dad was one of seven siblings, the eighth being my Uncle Mark, who had passed away. My Grandma Coleman and Grandpa Coleman are buried next to my Uncle Mark's grave.

That house soon became my childhood home. We moved in on Christmas Eve, as our old house sold faster than expected. We were almost homeless, but luckily, we could move into the new house within a couple of days of leaving the old one. Friends from church helped my parents move quickly in the cold and wet weather. My mom carefully kept an eye on the Christmas tree and the bag of wrapped presents to ensure nothing got lost in the moving shuffle.

While people went back and forth trying to empty the old house in as few trips as possible, my mom was at the new house, guiding everyone on where to put things. While directing traffic, she also assembled the Christmas tree. She was adamant that we would still have a magical Christmas even though the house was in chaos. My older siblings worked quickly to get the house in some kind of order. Eric and I were still so little that we were no help, so we stayed out of the way, arguing over which room we would get. It was the first time since I was young that I would have my own room again. I hated sharing a room with not only my brother but also a boy. He had no respect for my things and was the most annoying human being alive. Our sibling rivalry only grew stronger with time.

When we were small enough to be carried around, on Christmas morning, our parents would come into our rooms while we were still groggy. My dad would carry me, and my mom would carry my brother to the living room. As we got older, we walked down the stairs slowly, rubbing our eyes and yawning. But once we realized it was Christmas morning, excitement replaced our sleepiness.

When I was young, my older sister Brooke would often have to wake me up. She'd come into my room, gently rub my back, and softly tell me it was time to get up. She'd repeat until she saw me shift or make a noise. Then she'd leave, thinking I was awake, but she was wrong. She'd come back and try again, but I still wouldn't budge. Finally, after trying to be gentle, she'd pull me, thinking I was pretending to sleep. The moment she stood me up, I fell straight to the floor, all my body weight crashing down at once. I woke up crying because it felt like I had fallen out of bed. My sister felt terrible and still does. As I got older, no one wanted the task of waking me up anymore. It wasn't until my preteen years that I finally got myself up; thanks to a blaring alarm clock.

Christmas morning came, and we awoke with excitement, reassured that Santa had come, even though we had switched houses at the last minute. It felt like a Christmas fairytale. The tree glowed with lights, and all our ornaments hung on its branches. The presents were neatly wrapped and placed around the tree. Eric and I were always the last to be awakened, so everything could be double-checked before we came and destroyed the room. Our siblings were all seated and waiting for us to come down the stairs. My mom watched anxiously to see our reactions as we unwrapped each gift while my dad sat on the couch with his morning coffee, smiling.

It became a running joke that even though every present read "From Mom & Dad," my dad had no idea what was inside. After opening gifts, we'd thank both parents, and my dad would just smile and raise his coffee cup like a toast, or give me a look that said he was trying to hide the fact that he had no clue what I was opening.

Each year, someone in our family was chosen to be "Santa." Usually, it was my sister Brooke or me. We'd get into our organizational mode, stacking three or four presents next to each person. Since I still wasn't an early riser and Eric was too focused on his own gifts, Brooke usually played "Santa." She kept the role for a couple more years until it was unanimously decided that the youngest should take over. I held the job for a while until Eric eventually did. We always got everything we wanted and more. It was the first of many Christmases in what became the Coleman house.

Truthfully, what I was most excited about was finally having my own room. The door didn't lock, but I could still shut it in my brother's face.

My childhood home was a little difficult to get used to at first, since it had always been my grandma's house for as long as I could remember. It was also strange because, when I visited before, there were rooms that were "off limits." The rooms we were allowed to play in had names like the "Beanie Baby Room," "Eagle Room," "Tan Room," and my Grandma's Room. So, being able to open every door and explore every corner felt exciting and new.

When it was my grandma's house, every closet was packed with clothes neatly hung on wire hangers, each covered with a plastic bag to keep them clean. She always dressed to the nines. Even when going to McDonald's, she'd wear a dress, skirt, blouse, and matching coat, complete with heels, earrings, and a necklace. My grandma also had a signature perfume that had a distinct "grandma smell." Her hair was always perfectly styled in a perm.

Prior to our moving in, the house was decorated like it was from the 1960s. She loved all things plants, flowers, and greenery. The basement seating area was covered in vines and plants, almost like her own greenhouse. My cousins and I would pretend we were in a forest. Sometimes we didn't want to go down there because of the spiders.

Grandma had a deck that extended into a second deck with a long built-in bench. She kept flower boxes and even used an old tractor seat as decoration and extra seating. The railing had three boards, and a swinging bench sat closest to the house. The yard wasn't long but was quite wide. Tall plants grew all around the deck, and to reach the waterspout, you had to walk through what we called "the forest," full of spiders and bugs. This was before the days of quarterly pest control, so we regularly saw ants, spiders, and roly-polies.

Her backyard was mostly open grass beyond the plants and flowers. On the right side, a door led into the garage, and another near the waterspout led into the basement. The giant deck was made entirely of wood and lasted for years.

When the house was finally emptied, and my grandma's belongings were distributed or donated, it became an empty canvas for my mom to let her creativity shine, while still keeping the integrity of the home's original structure.

Our childhood home had five main bedrooms upstairs and potentially another in the basement. There were three full bathrooms and one half bath: two upstairs, one half bath on the main floor, and one full bath in the basement.

When you first walked in, the entryway had marble flooring. Immediately to the left were two hall closets, and between them was the entrance to the living room. Beyond the living room, with its giant glass window overlooking the front yard, was the dining room. The dining room led to the open-concept kitchen, which connected to the family room. From there, doors led to the garage and backyard. Near the family room, a stairway went down to the finished basement.

The basement had a large recreation room with an adjacent sitting area, a built-in half bar, a laundry room, a full bathroom, and the extra bedroom that became our homeschool classroom. Over the years, the room served many purposes; from a ping pong table and foosball area to a gaming room and later my dad's naptime hideaway. It housed graduation and birthday parties, and even my sister's church youth group meetings.

The final setup included a pool table, my grandma's piano (which took four men to move), and my dad's speaker system. When the piano was eventually dismantled, my dad made coat racks for each of Grandma's grandkids. A beautiful way to preserve a piece of her.

At the top of the stairs, directly ahead was a bathroom with double sinks. To the right was Brooke's room, which used to be my grandma's. Next to it was the master bedroom, my parents' room with a door leading to a balcony. Down the hallway were three more bedrooms. Mine, which had been the "Tan Room," Eric's, which was the "Beanie Baby Room," and a guest room that my sister Natalie used when she stayed with us.

This home became my mom's ongoing project for years. She knocked down the wall between the kitchen and dining room and replaced the old carpet with new flooring. Slowly, the house transformed, decorated with touches of Grandma's style and modern updates.

Adjusting to our new home came easier once we saw it in a different light. I missed our old neighbors, but I loved living in a bigger house and meeting new friends. There were plenty of kids nearby. Antioch Middle School, part of the Shawnee Mission School District (SMSD), was just a street away. Many older neighbors already knew my grandma and even remembered my dad as a little boy. That made it easy to feel at home.

Within the next couple of years, life remained busy. My dad worked as a railway engineer for Kansas City Southern Railway. He had been laid off from BNSF and quickly picked up by KCS when I was too young to remember the change. To supplement our income, my dad cleaned make-ready apartments and handled maintenance for a nearby complex. The perks? We got to use the apartment pool for free.

Because we were homeschooled, we often went with my mom while she cleaned apartments. Sometimes, we all pitched in to meet deadlines.

As for me, I was involved in everything my parents enrolled us in: the summer swim team with Overland Park (OP) Waves, Summer Bowling league at Mission Bowl, and church activities like Missionettes—the Christian version of Girl Scouts. I excelled in school, loved reading, and even taught myself to speed-read. I dreamed of joining the National Spelling Bee and practiced by memorizing words from a dictionary and using them in everyday conversations.

I even learned the first 20 U.S. presidents to the tune of "Twinkle Twinkle Little Star." Did that help in eighth-grade history quizzes? Absolutely. I was determined to "be somebody." I wanted to be a world changer. Life between ages six and fourteen felt blissful and simple; full of opportunity, and untouched by judgment.

Although those years were mostly happy, I still received occasional comments about my ethnicity, the kind that made me painfully aware that I looked different from my parents. People would ask my mom, "Is her father Chinese?" or joke, "Chinese right? Are you worried they put a chip in her head and someday China will push a button, and she will kill us all?" Even as a child, those words cut deep.

My mom always handled it with humor. She'd reply. "No, her father's tall, white, and German." Or "I don't know, I've never met him." Once, she even said, "One in every three is Chinese, so it was bound to happen sometime."

People often compared my mom to Angelina Jolie, who had recently adopted children herself. Over time, these comments became so routine that when I introduced myself, I'd preemptively explain why I was Chinese and my parents weren't or why I spoke perfect English. I even found myself explaining my name before anyone could ask.

By 2005, life had settled into a calm rhythm. I loved homeschooling, and Eric was my built-in best friend. My older siblings were busy with their teenage lives, so we would mostly see them at home occasionally. Whenever Brooke came home, I would rush to her room, eager to be part of everything she was doing. But she needed her privacy, so I was usually kicked out, left pouting at her closed door.

Turning around, I'd find my alternative, Eric, lying perfectly still on his life-size Bob the Builder puzzle, watching TV. I'd sigh, roll my eyes, and sit next to him.

Eric was a great playmate, but I wanted a girl to play with. Whenever he played with Barbies with me, he only used his GI Joes, who would destroy my Barbies in mortal combat. I was meticulous with my toys, always keeping them neat and clean. Once I got a doctor's kit for Christmas and wanted to play doctor, Eric, of course, used the stethoscope as a weapon and chased me with it. If I dared to look back, I'd be met with a smack to the face. It was always a race to see who could strike last before Mom caught us and punished us both equally.

That was our daily rhythm—safe, familiar, and full of mischief. It didn't matter where we came from or that we didn't look like our parents. We had a mom, dad, and siblings—and that was enough.

One day, that innocent bubble burst a little. My mom took us to the beloved Toys "R" Us, sometimes as a treat, sometimes just to browse. As we walked through the aisles, I stopped abruptly in front of a wall of Barbies. My mom turned and looked at me, puzzled. She followed my gaze and saw the endless rows of neatly boxed Barbies and Kens.

I looked up at her and asked, "Mom, why are all the Barbies and Kens white?"

Her face softened, and she said quietly, "I'm sorry, Autumn."

Tears welled in my eyes. None of those dolls looked like me. They all had the same pale skin and shades of blonde, brown, or red hair. I told her, "I don't want to play with Barbies anymore."

She hugged me tightly, her perfume comforting and familiar. "Let's go down another aisle," she said gently. "Maybe you'll find something new."

Determined, I followed her—and that's when I saw her: a doll with sleek black hair, bright red lips, almond-shaped eyes, and high-heeled boots. Her name was Jade, part of the original Bratz collection. She was different—confident, bold, and beautiful.

Jade became my new favorite doll, and the Bratz collection became my world. They didn't erase the hurt entirely, but they helped me see beauty that looked a little more like mine. Eric wouldn't dare touch them. I kept them perfect, their hair smooth, their clothes immaculate. For the first time, I felt seen.

Chapter 6:
Faith in Motion

I played alone when it came to my Bratz dolls. But if I wanted to play video games or have someone play the superhero while I was the "damsel in distress" or his sidekick, I played with Eric. One sunny afternoon, my mom was driving home when something familiar stirred inside her. As she stopped at a sign, a calm but unmistakable voice spoke to her once again. She felt God tell her it was time to adopt, but this time, for an older child, one not considered "normal" in the eyes of China.

She sat there quietly, letting the message sink in as if the world had frozen around her. When she got home, she told my dad what she had felt. He gave her the same look he'd given twice before, the one that said she must be out of her mind. Two adoptions already felt like plenty, and both Eric and I were a handful. They certainly didn't have money for another child.

But my mom's expression hardened with determination. Twice before, she'd let that voice go unanswered, and standing behind her, the living reminders of what obedience had brought, Eric and I, listening curiously to their conversation. My dad sighed and said what he would soon regret, "If you can make it happen, then so be it." I've learned never to say those words to my mother unless you want an "I told you so."

At the time, my mom had a close-knit circle of homeschooling friends, including Suzanne, a math teacher who homeschooled her youngest son. Suzanne often babysat us when Mom was busy and helped me with my math lesson. She had a side business in her basement, selling prom dresses. What began as a small project had grown into something real; she'd eventually own her own store with staff. Back then, she had just one employee, and we often tagged along on her shopping trips to the malls and outlets searching for discounted or out-of-season gowns. She would then take them home, repair or style them, and sell them on the up-and-coming eBay website. I loved being surrounded by all those dresses, and Suzanne would become a vital part of helping my mom raise the funds for our adoption.

As the paperwork and home study began, Mom threw herself into finding ways to afford the process. Some people criticized her, saying, "If you don't have the funds to adopt, you shouldn't be doing it." She would fire back, "If insurance companies didn't cover most of childbirth, then women wouldn't be having children either." Adoption cost thousands, but Mom had a stubborn determination that matched her faith. She took over Dad's apartment-cleaning side business, cleaning new units every night. Every dollar mattered.

She also enlisted Suzanne's help. Together, they made a deal with an apartment complex that admired Mom's work ethic: she could rent the clubhouse for a weekend. They gathered prom dresses by the hundreds from stores thanks to Suzanne's relationships with local shop owners. My mom advertised the sale everywhere, billboards, grass signs, even stapled flyers next to "missing puppy" posters on wooden poles that lined the streets. (Those poles, still standing today, must hold thousands of rusted staples in their grooves.)

Eric and I, ages eight and nine, helped however we could. My older sister, always the one with the giving heart, was there too. Rows upon rows of dresses filled the clubhouse, organized by style, color, and size. As we waited for the doors to open, Mom prayed quietly, asking God to provide the last few thousand she needed.

At first, customers would trickle in. Then the beeps of the opening door became constant. Shoppers crowded the clubhouse, trying on dresses in the restroom, admiring gowns, and laughing with excitement. Suzanne managed the sales like a pro, and my sister worked the cash register while we kids collected hangers.

By the end of the first day, exhaustion set in. But Mom's faith didn't waver. She prayed again that night, thanking God for whatever was to come. The next morning, as sunlight poured through the windows, the beeps began again, and they didn't stop. Dress after dress was sold. The racks that had been packed full were nearly empty by closing time.

Hiding beneath one of those racks, I watched my mom smile on the outside while her eyes betrayed her worry. I whispered a prayer of my own: that God would help her raise the money, not just because of her adoption, but because she had worked so hard. When they counted the money that evening, I saw tears fill her eyes. She had done it. Against all odds, she'd raised the last of the funds she needed.

Mom thanked Suzanne and everyone who had helped, packed everything up, and went home, without stopping, without distractions. She handed my dad the heavy bank bag full of cash, a triumphant grin on her face. My dad, sitting in his chair with his coffee and newspaper, looked at her in disbelief. She crossed her arms, waiting for him to speak. Finally, he chuckled and said, "Well, looks like we're going to China?" That's how my mom operates, quiet determination, then victory.

This time, she requested a little girl from China who was older than a toddler and had the same medical situation as Eric. When my brother was adopted, they'd learned about his special health needs, still without a cure today. Because Mom knew how to navigate his medical care, she wanted to give another child with the same condition a home.

One day, while mailing documents to China, a man behind her noticed the address and struck up a conversation. His wife, Helena, was from China. They soon became friends, and Helena offered to help. When my mom finally received the photo of the girl who would become my little sister, I remember studying it closely, her short, uneven hair, her serious expression, and those deep brown eyes that seemed to have already seen too much.

Mom made her a photo book filled with pictures of our house, pets, and family. On the back of each photo, she wrote handwritten notes in her near-cursive. My sister's new room was purple with green floral accents, a bright rug in the center, and white-painted furniture. "Everything's ready," Mom said. "All we needed is her," is what my mom used to say.

This time, I was ten, old enough to remember everything, and I got to go to China with my mom.

September 2006 arrived quietly, like the first leaf of fall, sudden yet expected. Mom had packed weeks in advance, suitcases neatly lined by the front door. We boarded our flight to Beijing, where Helena's friend met us to be our guide.

That trip was unforgettable. From Tiananmen Square and the Forbidden City to the Great Wall of China, every sight felt monumental. Beijing was buzzing with preparation for the 2008 Olympics; I even saw the Bird's Nest Stadium as it was being built. The Olympic mascots were everywhere: Beibei the fish, Jingjing the panda, Yingying the antelope, Nini the swallow, and Huanhuan the flame. Mom bought me a keychain with all of them. It still hangs from my rearview mirror today, faded but cherished.

Walking the Great Wall was surreal. In history books, it looks impossibly steep, but in some areas, the ground had shifted over time. It stretched endlessly, 131,171 miles of stone and history.

At one point, Mom decided to rest at a tower while our guide offered to keep walking with me. After a few towers, the guide stopped to buy water. I waited until I didn't. Somehow, I convinced myself she'd gone ahead, and I needed to catch up. Within minutes, I was lost on the Great Wall of China.

Panic hit. My mind raced through absurd scenarios: I'd have to learn Chinese, beg on the streets, never see my family again. I thought I blended in, but to locals, I screamed American. Eventually, I started back down, retracing my steps until I spotted Mom talking with an elderly man. When I tried to interrupt, she held up her finger and said, "Don't interrupt." I waited, then blurted out what happened.

When the guide finally appeared hours later, she was furious and relieved all at once. Turns out she'd told me to stay put, turned around, and I was gone. My mom apologized, then gave me the look. Even in another country, her look traveled well. Lesson learned.

Before leaving Beijing, we dined at a restaurant famous for its Peking duck, accessible only by rickshaw. It was incredible—but very different from "Chinese food" back home. There were no fortune cookies or beef and broccoli, but plenty of bok choy, seafood, and… unsettling sights. Once, in a market, two men walked past carrying what I thought was a Great Dane—until Mom quietly confirmed it was a dog being prepared for roasting. That night, she explained gently that in China, dog meat is as normal as pork in the U.S. I vowed then to eat only noodles, dumplings, rice, and McDonald's for the rest of the trip.

From Beijing, we flew to Changsha in Hunan Province to meet my little sister. The process wasn't as welcoming as before; by 2006, foreign adoptions were more scrutinized. People stared. Restaurants hesitated to serve us.

At the government building, I sat with the video camera pointed out the window, counting potholes out of boredom. Then, a van pulled up. Two women stepped out with a little girl between them—white capris, striped shirt, short hair sticking out every which way. My mom started sobbing before the girl even reached us.

The child looked up and said, "My name is Jennifer Coleman." My mom cried harder, replying, "I'm Mama." She pointed to me: "Jie Jie," big sister. Jennifer smiled. From that moment, she was ours.

We toured China together, shopping at a two-story Wal-Mart with knockoff "Aeropostale" clothes, visiting parks filled with bronze statues of children. Jennifer and I wore matching outfits and held hands everywhere we went. She never looked back, never hesitated. That kind of trust, I now realize, must have taken immense courage.

In Guangzhou, we finalized the adoption at the White Swan Hotel, where Jennifer received her "lucky" Barbie with a tiny Chinese baby. Nearby, we visited a park called The American Dream, where statues of plump Americans and their equally round dogs lined the path. My mom posed beside one, mimicking the stance for a photo, her humor shining through even in moments of discomfort.

At one hotel, I looked out our window into a classroom across the alley. Rows of uniformed children sat at their desks, studying quietly, the teacher writing on a chalkboard. It hit me—had I stayed in China, that wouldn't have been my life. Orphaned children didn't go to school like that. Watching them, I felt both grateful and sad.

Our time in China ended with the Mid-Autumn Moon Festival. Fireworks exploded outside our window, and the streets filled with laughter, lanterns, and the smell of mooncakes. Jennifer soaked in every moment with wonder. She was brave, kind, and stubborn, the perfect fit for our family.

When we returned home, Dad was waiting at the airport with open arms. Expecting her to be afraid, he bent down gently, but Jennifer ran to him, kissed his cheek, and said, "Ni Hao, Baba." Tears filled his eyes.

That was the moment we all understood the meaning of complete.

Looking back, both adoption journeys were blessings. Seeing where I came from should have brought peace, but instead, I buried those memories. I shoved away the pain and the wonder, treating those trips as if they were ordinary vacations. I didn't allow myself to feel the depth of it all. I pushed down the hurt, the confusion, and the identity questions until they shaped a version of me I barely recognized.

Chapter 7:
Finding My Voice

As Jennifer's adoption settled into place and the year of 8th grade approached, I found myself longing for something I had only heard about from my friends at church: the everyday chatter of public school. I wanted to experience it firsthand. I confided in a close friend about how to approach my parents and ask them to attend public school. She gave me tips on presenting it in a way that made them more likely to say yes.

My parents were not a fan of public schooling, especially after my kindergarten experiences. The way I had been treated seven years prior still lingered in their minds. But I was anxious to go and to "fit in" to speak the language of those who had attended public school all along. Kindergarten had faded into my distant memory, and I assumed I would never see those kids again. My mom eventually told me that I could go if I kept one promise. To which I agreed. The promise was to remain who I was and not let outside influences change my behavior for the worse. I was to remember to believe in God and not to disown him to fit in.

Before Eric and I could start public school, we took placement tests to determine our grades. Both of us scored higher than our ages suggested. I had the option to skip ahead to high school freshman year, while Eric could start 7th Grade. On the first day, eager but nervous, I decided to stay with my age group, enrolling in Antioch Middle School from August 2009 to May 2010. Eric began 6th grade at Antioch Elementary School. I was excited to meet new friends, but shy about how they would react to a girl who hadn't grown up with them.

To my surprise, I ran into my best friends from kindergarten. I had never expected to see familiar faces from those early years. When I saw Beck, we smiled at each other, not immediately remembering the inseparable bond we once had. After a few moments, we focused back on class, the recognition lingering silently. After a familiar face emerged, Nicolette, the tall blonde girl with daily pigtails, whose house I used to visit. My nervousness melted away. The worry that there were visible differences between us.

As the weeks passed, the awkwardness dissolved. We traced our connections back to kindergarten, laughing at the shared memories. Seeing Beck, I understood what he must have wondered silently: Where had I disappeared to for seven years? I avoided answering; some memories were buried for a reason. They had served their purpose, and now they were gone.

Middle school operated on a schedule drastically different from what I had known. Each class had a strict time before the bell, and teachers often ran over or rushed through lessons. Assigned seats expedited attendance, and lunch periods were short enough that I learned to eat quickly or throw food away. Odd and even classes' schedules rotated daily, a preparation for high school's structure. Middle school felt like a constant race to absorb as much knowledge as possible. I sympathized with teachers, knowing forty-five minutes was rarely enough to reach every student. Yet, I quickly grew to love the school environment.

My homeschooling experience has been invaluable. My mother had done her best, navigating curricula that weren't always her strength, especially in math. But middle school teachers ignited something new in me. They became mentors I admired, from gym teachers to the school nurse. I loved learning from them, not just the subjects they taught, but who they were.

One teacher who left a lasting impression was Mr. Mosbie, my Algebra teacher. I came in expecting to hate math, a subject I had long struggled with. But he taught not by dictation but by sparking curiosity, encouraging me to ask questions and explore answers on my own. Numbers came alive on the page; concepts clicked in ways I had never experienced. I could almost see them arranging themselves into solutions, like a puzzle falling into place. I would later pursue a degree in mathematics, thanks in large part to his guidance.

Equally memorable was Mrs. Shray, my English teacher. Small in stature but immense in presence, she commanded respect and nurtured discipline without cruelty. With the help of Mrs. Nova, her classroom assistant, she fostered my love for literature and taught me to stand up for myself. These women shaped my voice and confidence in ways I carry to this day.

Of course, middle school was not without challenges. The arrogance and egotism I had thought I left behind in kindergarten resurfaced, this time in the form of pre-teen boys obsessed with image and dominance. Axe cologne, faux chocolate scents, and barely-there mustaches accompanied their attempts to assert "manhood." I endured racist and cruel remarks and jabs at my ethnicity, my adoption, and my upbringing.

By 8th grade, my patience wore thin. I snapped back at insults with words that cut deep. I called out broken homes, lack of class, and poverty with the force of someone who had been pushed to the edge. I became a bully in retaliation, instilling fear in those who had mocked me. Though I felt protected and empowered in the moment, I later understood that defending oneself does not justify tearing others down. This was a hard, formative lesson—one that taught me about the consequences of hurt, both given and received.

The year ended with the chaos of yearbooks and farewell notes. H.A.G.S., "Have a great summer," filled pages alongside heartfelt messages from friends and teachers. Even the kindergarten "mean girls" left their marks, though they seemed unaware of past grievances. Middle school had been a mix of cringe-worthy moments, social rivalries, and awkward adolescent hierarchies. Girls and boys seemed to inhabit different worlds, navigating trends like moccasins, Sperrys, The North Face, and Abercrombie.

On the final day, while signing yearbooks on the front lawn, I met someone new—Axel, whose story about gum in his hair prompted a teasing remark from me about his haircut. Laughter followed, and we parted for the summer, unaware of what high school would bring. Walking home, I felt a mix of relief, accomplishment, and trepidation. Eighth grade was over, and a new chapter loomed ahead.

Chapter 8:
Where I Came From

High school is the stage in life where you officially become a teenager. It's where identity begins to take shape, where independence is formed or withheld, for some. That morning, I took deep breaths and hoped to see friends I had not seen since the previous school year, only three months ago, but to adolescents, it feels like an eternity. I prepped early. I wore a cute, floral, mid-length skirt with a soft purple tank top covered by a dark pink, short-sleeved pullover to hide my exposed shoulders. I slipped on my flats and grabbed the one-shoulder, waist-length bag my mom had made me. It was black and white on the outside; inside, it was red with pandas. We'd been told we didn't need backpacks on the first day, just a day of activities to get used to everything.

I stepped outside and waited patiently for the bus. In middle school, I'd walked because it was just up the street. When the bus pulled up, I climbed aboard and greeted the driver. She smiled and returned it. I sat in the second seat from the front on the right. Most kids chose as far away from the bus driver as possible, but I knew mine. I knew all the drivers in the Shawnee Mission School District (SMSD). When my siblings and I started public school, my mom became a bus driver so she could be off when we were and still bring in income. It wasn't unusual for me to spend time with her and the other bus drivers. As the bus neared the school, an adrenaline rush hit me. Part of me was still tired; high school started much earlier than middle school. Another part wondered whether the friends I'd once known would pretend not to recognize me. I stepped off the bus, wished my driver a wonderful day, and started in my new world.

My school was enormous compared to my old one. It seemed endless. Shawnee Mission North High School (SMN), home of the Indians, had the mascot at the time. Inside the gymnasium, I recognized many from middle school, and just as many I didn't. I took a seat and watched students file in. Some greeted each other like they'd been together the day before. Some stood to announce their presence. Others talked about their summer adventures. A few sat awkwardly, staring at all the commotion. Then one of my middle school friends spotted me and came over. Her name was Kendra. She was, and still is, sweet. We'd spent many days together the year before, so her presence softened the edges of my nerves.

The assembly began. The next four years of our lives started right there in that gym. We were divided into groups and sent through the school for presentations and tours. Seniors guided us as we wandered, most of us bumping into people or walls because we were hyper-focused on the tiny schedule papers in our hands. By the end, it felt like I'd walked across Egypt. Middle school had been simple: seventh grade on the first floor, eighth on the second. Lockers matched your grade. The gym, cafeteria, library, and electives all lived on the first floor. High school was a maze.

As I sat there absorbing the "norms" and the "traditions," I thought, "This is it. This is where I discover who I'm meant to be." I imagined the blank pages of my future laid out in front of me, waiting to be written on. My heart thudded with purpose. No one felt more determined than I did. I wanted to make my mark, to do what I believed I'd been adopted for, to give back to a world that had given me a second chance at life.

The first weeks of freshman year were quiet. Everyone was still learning schedules, now mixed with three older grades rushing through the halls. They were always packed. I felt like I spent half my time running and the other half memorizing bathroom locations. It was a universal understanding that freshmen stayed quiet. You were at the bottom of the food chain. You didn't draw attention to yourself with unnecessary boldness.

My teachers were wonderful, every single one. I still remember them all by name. Building relationships with them came easily. Making friends with peers did not. When it came time to choose classes, my mom encouraged me to enroll in something she'd once loved. I had my heart set on culinary and baking. I dreamed of becoming a pastry chef. But she urged me to try one class, just for freshman year. If I hated it, I wouldn't have to continue. Reluctantly, I agreed. The class was Naval Junior Reserve Officer Training Corps (NJROTC). As I sat at my desk, wondering what this class even involved, a swift figure entered the room. He moved past the desks with a pace only a cheetah could rival. I didn't even see where he came from.

We stood for the Pledge of Allegiance and then took our seats. Roll call followed, absent or present. I was terrified. The man standing was short compared to my dad. His hair was cut in a strict military high-and-tight. He wore a pullover cardigan, tan slacks, and black dress shoes polished so well you could see your reflection in them. When he spoke, his voice was hoarse yet confident, as if he had spent years projecting orders across open fields. He could silence a room in half a second. A hallway, even. He was built solid, well within military height and weight standards. Little did I know then that this man would shape all four years of my high school life, and beyond.

His name was Mr. Gray. To this day, I call him "Grand Master G," though that nickname wasn't allowed until much later. He explained the program, what it demanded, what it promised, and how it would mold us. He kept referring to us as "young Americans." It wasn't the only phrase he became known for, but it was first. As he paced back and forth, his conviction filled the room. He believed in every word he spoke. The way we tracked him with our eyes, I was certain we would've followed him into battle, though I had no idea what that battle might be. Another name soon became just as familiar: "Chief." He was never called anything else. Chief Nevel, Chief Petty Officer, United States Navy, Retired. Mr. Gray was a Chief Warrant Officer 4, United States Marine Corps, Retired. Both men bore rows of medals and carried stories that could fill books. I admired them deeply. I still do. And so it began, the race to the finish line.

Freshman year was mostly about learning routines: how classrooms worked. How teachers operated, how to exist in this new academic ecosystem. I had no interest in dances or dating. Or so I thought. Behind me in every ROTC class sat Axel, the kid whose horrible haircut I once commented on. He used to flick his hair out of his eyes with a sharp twist of his head. It was exhausting to watch. But in ROTC, all males were required to get high-and-tights. Females wore sock buns or kept their hair above the collar. Individuality dissolved. You could identify a cadet by their haircut alone. Then by their posture. No ROTC cadet was allowed to get in trouble elsewhere without Mr. Gray finding out. There was no detention or a trip to the principal. You were sent to him. And whatever followed was far worse.

After Axel got his haircut, learned what cologne was (not Axe), dissolved the importance of daily showers, and changed his socks regularly, he became my friend. One of my best friends. Not long after, we started dating, the very thing I swore off that first morning. I really need to stop making promises I can't keep. I put him through the wringer. I was on a mission. He was either on the boat or he could jump off. I had goals, dreams, and ambitions. I was going to do something great. I joined other activities, like the girls' swim team, but ROTC became my center. Ranking higher and higher was an adrenaline rush. I wanted to be the best. I wanted to be "the favorite" in Mr. Gray's eyes.

My hunger for outward acceptance turned me into a "hard charger." I followed directions flawlessly. When I failed, I took it personally. I practiced relentlessly. No wishing on stars or Disney magic was going to build my future. For the first time, I felt purpose. Everything aligned into a straight, unwavering path: perfect grades and perfection in Mr. Gray's eyes. I joined Athletic, Drill, Academic, and later Color Guard teams. What my mom had suggested as a 'trial' became my entire world. ROTC felt like home. A family of "young Americans" striving toward the same goal.

Outside of it, I had to face the rest of high school, students who saw structure and uniformity as ridiculous. Wanting to wear a uniform at school baffled them. The halls were lined with your groups and cliques, though North wasn't quite the jungle portrayed in movies. It was more fluid, more blended, a melting pot of interest and cultures. Racially, though, Asians were a small minority. The student body was primarily white, Black, and Hispanic. There were a few Asians, Chinese in particular, and I didn't relate to them anyway. I had already distanced myself from my heritage. It didn't bother me that I was a minority. My friends treated me as an exception. I didn't "sound Asian." I didn't dress like one. I didn't have Asian parents. And I had the whitest name imaginable. It became easy to forget I was Asian at all.

In truth, it felt safer not to associate with Asians. Doing so had only ever led to bullying. I stayed within ROTC and with classmates I felt comfortable around. Yet even after disowning my own race, the isolation followed me. What I thought I had left behind in kindergarten and middle school simply came with me. Surely it would end someday. Right? Instead, I grew colder and darker. With every comment about my looks, I began to resent Asians, myself included. I started making racist jokes about my own race. That gave others permission to do the same. Because I "removed" myself from that category, I convinced myself it didn't feel hurt. In fact, I felt numb.

The only time I embraced being Asian was when it earned me a compliment. Otherwise, I weaponized it. If I made the joke first, no one else could hurt me with it. Or so I thought. But the comments kept coming, like a tsunami flooding hallways, pinning me against lockers. I hated my birth parents; I hated everything tied to abandonment. I belonged *here,* and I was white. This belief might as well have been stamped on my forehead. I blurted it out in introductions to new people, as if saying it enough times would make it true.

One of the core subjects in high school is history. Within it are lessons on the wars that shaped nations and the role the United States played throughout them. Among those lessons is Pearl Harbor, the buildup, the tension, the timeline of events that led to December 7, 1941, and finally the bombing itself.

Because of the attack's brutality and its significance in American history, Pearl Harbor Remembrance Day exists. Each year on December 7th, teachers pause not only to remember but to teach why the day matters and why it must not be forgotten.

To many young, immature boys, history itself is already unbearable. Instead of listening, they fill their empty brain space by drawing cruel, ignorant lines between Pearl Harbor and the modern Asian population.

More than once, boys approached me and said, "It's because of you Japs that we have to learn about this stupid holiday."

They meant Pearl Harbor Remembrance Day, if the "holiday" part of their statement wasn't obvious enough.

My immediate reaction was violent. Prison-level violent. Beating them senseless felt like the only rational response. If I got my hands on them, they wouldn't walk away.

Instead, I stood there, staring, trying to find even a sliver of 'benefit of the doubt' to explain their stupidity.

There was none.

One day, a white boy said it to me again. He stood there smug, proud of himself, as if he'd just delivered a masterful burn.

I replied calmly, "You have it wrong."

He blinked, replaying his words in his head, certain he said exactly what he meant. Then he repeated himself.

"I heard you the first time." I said, "I am telling you; you've got it wrong."

He smirked and glanced around to see if anyone was watching, "How so?"

He looked confident, certain that nothing I said could match the insult he believed he'd delivered. I stood in silence, letting responses scroll through my mind like a camera roll.

Then I decided: if he was going to waste my time, I would at least give him a proper history lesson.

I began, "You say 'japs,'" making air quotes. "First of all, Japanese people are not 'japs.' That's a degrading term born from a specific moment in history, Pearl Harbor, and everything surrounding it. Second, I am not Japanese. I am Chinese."

He opened his mouth to interrupt.

I raised my finger and said, "Finally, I was not born, pre-conceived, conceived, or even a distant thought in 1941. So your careless, half-formed dig, and your warped sense of history, don't offend me. They humiliate you."

I paused to breathe. His smug expression faltered as his brain worked overtime to keep up.

Then I continued.

"I almost feel bad that a romantic night led to your conception in vain. Because instead of producing an intelligent, kind, and thoughtful human, they ended up with an egotistical, misogynistic, racist asshole for a son, who looks like he needs to put more brain cells towards learning about history rather than smoking it."

He stared at me, stunned. I held his gaze, giving him the chance to say something, anything.

When he didn't, I rolled my eyes.

"If you have nothing else to insult me with," I said, "get the fuck out of my way."

I shoved past him and walked on, feeling a surge of pride at what I'd just done.

But inside, something cracked.

Because this was my life, insults answered by insults, battles in hallways instead of conversations. It felt as though a meaningful connection was something I would never be allowed to have.

In many of my classes, most of which were filled with boys, their lack of mental development showed itself through assumptions. Because I was Asian, I was automatically 'smart'. They aren't wrong in that I *was* very smart. But equating intelligence to my race was infuriating.

In math class, a boy sat to my left. He constantly tried to copy my work. What he didn't understand was that even with the correct answer, you still had to show how you got there. Without the process, the points didn't count.

I grew tired of feeling his eyes burn holes through my paper. One day, I turned to him and told him to knock it off.

He glared at me, more offended at being caught than at what he was doing. Then he leaned closer and whispered that he'd give me Skittles from the bag on his desk if I'd just let him see.

I was insulted that a handful of candy was considered fair currency for my work.

"Choke on them," I snapped.

We both grew heated. Then he said it, loudly.

"You're the one who's fucking Chinese and knows math."

Every head in the room lifted. The air shifted. Even students who had been focused on the board froze.

Our teacher, Mr. Devins, had been calmly teaching. I wish I could thank him today for what he *allowed* in that moment. I don't know the rules teachers must follow, but I hope I don't get him in trouble for being a good human.

He turned sharply.

He looked at the boy. Then at me.

My stomach dropped. I was certain I would be the one in trouble. Sweat formed on my forehead. The boy looked proud.

"Repeat what you just said," Mr. Devins told him.

The boy scoffed, emboldened.

"All I'm saying is she's sitting over there like a ching chong knowing the fucking answers while I have to work hard over here trying to get them."

I couldn't believe he repeated it so easily.

Mr. Devins scanned the room, then back, to two desks in the very front row. I felt myself shrinking. Tears pressed behind my eyes. But the boy wasn't done.

"I tried to give her Skittles to help a brother out," he continued, like he was performing. "But no. She's fucking greedy, just like all of them Chinese people are."

My vision blurred. I refused to blink, afraid the tears would spill. In an instant, I was no longer a high schooler in a math class. I was a kindergartner again, small, isolated, being sent away for making a scene.

My teacher set down his notepad, scanning the room before locking his gaze on me. Then he said words I had never heard before: "I'm so sorry, Autumn."

My head was already so low it might as well have been on the floor. Confused, I looked up.

"I'm sorry Autumn that you have to witness and hear these terrible things," he repeated.

I glanced around, wondering if anyone else was hearing the same apology. I gave him a small nod, a mix of gratitude and acknowledgement, doing my best to hold my composure.

The student next to me looked puzzled. Why was the teacher apologizing to *me*?

Mr. Devins turned to him.

"You should be ashamed of yourself."

I thought that would be the end. But this student, clutching the bag of Skittles, persisted, trying to justify his actions, attempting to explain his side. My teacher's astonishment was palpable; he could not believe this kid wasn't getting it.

Finally, Mr. Devins let out a slow sigh. "I have to step out of the classroom for just a moment." He said, "I am not responsible for what happens while I am gone. I expect you all to remain on your best behavior and not move from your seats."

He looked directly at me as he spoke. He said he needed to fill his cup at the water fountain, and he would be right back.

Then he added, carefully, "If one of you was to slap another, just know I don't condone it. But then again, I wouldn't know about it."

And with that, he left the room.

The class shifted. Students glanced at one another, then at me. I turned toward the boy beside me, still clutching his bag of Skittles. He looked bewildered.

"Would you mind giving me the Skittles?" I asked.

He smirked. "Oh, you want them now?"

"Yes," I said calmly. "I want to show you something."

He handed me the half-empty bag. Rolling his eyes, he asked, "What could you possibly want to show me?"

I gripped the top of the bag with my left hand, wound my arm back as far as it would go, and smacked him across the back of the head with as much force as I could from my seat.

"Ouch! What was that for?" he yelped.

"For being an asshole," I said, smiling as I dropped the Skittles onto his desk.

Just then, Mr. Devins walked back into the room and resumed teaching as if nothing had happened. No question. No glance. He simply picked up where he left off.

Looking back, I'm sure he never went far. He probably stood in the hallway, close enough to hear everything. I imagine him biting back laughter, already forming the story he'd tell at home about how his day went.

That student never asked me for anything again.

He never even looked in my direction.

One incident I remember vividly from high school happened at Oakland Mall, a prime hangout for teenagers. The area was packed with shops and restaurants, all designed to pull in crowds beyond the mall's food court. One restaurant, freshly arrived on the scene, was "TGI Fridays," *Thank God It's Fridays.*

Naturally, I was excited to try it, like every American teenager eager to be part of the latest food craze. And of course, we went on a Friday night, how fitting.

We were seated at a table in the middle of the restaurant, just enough room for my mom, my younger siblings, and me. As we flipped through the menus, unease started to creep in. The place was crowded, music blasting the latest hits. It had the vibe of a trendy, fashionable eatery while still claiming to be family-friendly, but for us, it felt anything but.

It was as if every pair of eyes in the restaurant were staring at us. Did we have something in our teeth? Were we underdressed? We have no idea. I leaned toward my mom. "Mom, people are staring at us."

She shrugged. "Pay them no mind. Just focus on what you want to order."

When our waiter finally came, he took our drink orders. My mom went first, then we all followed. But then, nothing. He didn't return for a long time. My mom started to fidget, growing impatient at the lack of service.

The waiter seemed younger, probably his first night on the job. He kept passing our table, helping others nearby. My mom muttered, "They must be very busy since it's the newest restaurant."

We sat there, feeling every gaze on us. My mom's discomfort grew, being watched like some exhibit at a zoo. Finally, she caught the attention of another waitress nearby, one helping a different table. She asked why our drinks hadn't arrived.

The waitress nodded and promised to check with whoever was assigned to our table.

As we waited, I noticed people speaking with their servers, then glancing toward our table. Over and over. My stomach tightened. Something wasn't right.

I braced myself for whatever awkward, painful conversation was coming when a man in a suit began walking toward us. He wore black slacks, a button-down shirt, and a tie. A headset clipped to his belt; an earpiece curled into his ear. He looked like someone who managed chaos for a living.

"I apologize," he said, "but several customers have voiced their concerns about their comfort regarding your… um… table."

He paused, waiting.

My head was facing toward him, but my eyes flicked past his shoulder, to the faces watching us, waiting.

"I don't understand what you mean by *our table*." My mom said calmly. "Please explain what you're insinuating?" She wasn't going to let him hide behind vagueness.

I grew restless. Eric's body stiffened, ready to explore. Jennifer colored quietly, blissfully unaware. I realized this moment would end one of two ways: either my mother would be escorted out in handcuffs, or we would be forced to leave.

The possibility of the manager standing up for us never truly crossed my mind.

It never does in situations like this.

"Well," he said carefully, "many of our guests are uncomfortable that you are going to be served… "

He gestured vaguely in our direction.

"Not because of *you*," he added.

My mom inhaled slowly. "You mean people are uncomfortable with my children because they are Asian?"

His face flushed. He glanced toward the exit and gestured with his hand.

"Please leave the building. It would be in everyone's best interest if you chose to dine elsewhere."

My mother stood, trembling with fury. She turned to the room and spoke loudly.

"I hope you're all happy. I hope you remember this moment, feeling threatened by children who did absolutely nothing to you. I hope it makes you proud to know you chose hatred today. Toward *children*."

She stood and told us to gather our things. We rose from our chairs in betrayal and shame. As we walked toward the exit, I locked eyes with every person who nodded in approval of our removal. My mom informed the room that she would be emailing both the owners and corporate about this experience.

Some people *clapped*.

That felt even more heinous. We never returned for obvious reasons. And, eventually, the restaurant closed.

My mom said gently, "There are many people who are uncomfortable with what they don't understand. They don't like people because of the color of their skin or the issues in the world. They don't like that we adopted you from your countries and brought you here."

Then she said something that etched itself into my memory: "There are people in this world who believe you belong where you came from."

Where did I come from?

I had been raised in the United States my entire life. I knew nothing else. The shock of that moment hollowed me. I felt ashamed of being American.

I watched Eric absorb it. I believe something clicked inside him that day—that there *was* a difference, that the world would sometimes remind him of it. I think part of his hardness grew from that moment. People often refuse to understand until they are forced to experience something themselves. Many stand for ideas they barely comprehend. And even those who say nothing, those who stay silent, become indistinguishable from those who shout. Silence is the true killer of joy, perspective, and understanding.

I can't speak for Eric's heart, but I remember looking at him during the drive home. None of us was hungry anymore. The rest of freshman year was relatively calm—at least in terms of bullying. Or maybe I was simply consumed by ROTC and competition. Sophomore year arrived quickly. I stayed focused, applied for a lifeguard position at Marshall Community Center, and was hired almost immediately. I would hold that job until the spring of 2014.

The world felt open. I was going to make something of myself. Classes were steady, teachers still incredible. Students settled into a routine. I poured myself into ROTC, even committing to summer programs that would help me advance in rank. Life felt aligned.

Church still felt good, too. I connected with friends there about public school—leaving out the parts about cussing and smacking boys with Skittles. That didn't fit neatly into my image of a Christian. Just as I compartmentalized my Asian identity, I compartmentalized my worlds. Church friends. School friends. ROTC Autumn. Sunday Autumn. I never mixed them. I lived in fragments and called it balance.

To this day, I still remember friends from church the same way I remember school friends. One who remains dearest to my heart is Cydney. We met at the age of three in her dad's Sunday School class. I was the kid who hid under tables and only came out when it was snack time.

One day, as I crouched beneath a table avoiding the world, someone crawled in beside me. I looked over. There she was—smiling. I smiled back. She didn't ask questions. She didn't wonder why I was hiding. She simply stayed.

From that moment on, we were inseparable.

Cydney was there for every major moment in my life. It wouldn't be right to tell this story without her. We did basketball, dance, and softball together. Even when she didn't participate, she showed up, cheering me on at swim meets. We were always at each other's houses. Truthfully, hers was the only home my mom would let me spend the night at anyway. Her family became my second family. I adored them.

There were others, too, Heather, Bethany, Evelyn, Mandy, and so many more who became permanent fixtures in my childhood memories. Most of these friendships lasted through high school. Eventually, as we all cross paths from time to time, we still follow one another online, quietly wishing each other well.

Still in sophomore year, school had become easier to navigate, even as the workload grew heavier. ROTC remained my sole focus. Each year brought a new challenge, but the ultimate goal never changed: win nationals.

Our final competition of the season was the Navy Nationals in Pensacola, Florida. Hundreds of schools competed throughout the year, all hoping to become one of the top twenty-five teams in the country. Mr. Gray had a reputation to uphold. Every year he had been an instructor, his cadets made it to nationals. You did not want to be the class that broke that streak. We worked relentlessly, and we made it.

We placed in the top five. We were proud. After the competition, we were allowed time to explore the beach and the city.

One evening, I walked along the shoreline. The sun had already set, and the ocean faded into darkness beyond what the hotel lights allowed us to see. Our hotel stood just steps from the sand. This was the only time we were permitted on the beach at night—just not in the water. Several of us wandered along the shore. Mr. Gray stood nearby, admiring the view.

A friend hurried up beside me.

"Hey," he said. "Mind if I walk with you?"

"Sure," I replied.

I didn't expect Charles to become a lifelong friend, but here we are—still in each other's lives. He studied me for a moment before asking, "Are you okay? You look upset."

"Nothing's wrong," I said. "Why would you think that?"

"I don't know," he said gently, "It just looks like something's bothering you."

I stopped walking and turned toward the ocean. I took a deep breath, closed my eyes, then slowly opened them. Charles mirrored me, then waited.

"Charles," I said, "all my life I've felt like I knew who I was. I've wanted to prove to the world that I was worth something. But now it's almost junior year, and before I know it, it will be graduation."

He nodded, trying to follow. "Okay… but what is your point?"

"Are you happy with what you've accomplished so far?"

His eyes dropped. No one had ever asked him that before. I had always been a deep thinker. I carved conversations that meant something.

"I am proud," he said slowly. "But I really want to figure my life out. Up to now, everything's been easy. I know I only have a couple of years left before life gets real."

I smiled. "Same. I'm tired of fighting people over things I can't control. I don't want to care anymore about what others think of my skin or my race. I don't want to keep making jokes just to survive. I've spent years hating myself to fit in—and I still don't belong."

He looked at me with empathy. "Then don't, Autumn. Stop trying to be someone you're not. Haters will always find reasons to hate. Don't hate yourself for them. You are who you are. Don't expect anything more from yourself than that."

His words settled into me.

"Look at me," he continued. "People see me as Mexican. My family is from Mexico. My parents speak Spanish. But I was born here. Do you think they see all that? No. They just see *me*—a Mexican who speaks Spanish. I could spend my life proving I'm more than that. Or I can prove it to myself."

I nodded and smiled. The sea breeze carried the scent of salt. I turned to him and said, "Thank you, Charles. Thank you for reminding me not to cower from who I am—but to shine in who I was meant to be."

He grinned, sensing the moment had grown heavy. "Hey, we brown people gotta stick together."

I laughed as his girlfriend approached. We brushed it off as "nothing serious," and he walked away with her. I stayed.

I closed my eyes and drifted back through time, kindergarten, middle school, every insult and racist comment. My hands curled into fists. I remembered the ways I had hurt others. The words I could never take back. I thought of my birth parents and how I had disowned them. Of everything I had done to make myself *less* Asian. Less Chinese. One by one, I handed each memory to the sea. My anger. My shame. My brokenness. My fear. My ignorance.

With every thought released, my fists loosened. The weight I carried grew lighter. I opened my eyes and made a quiet decision: I no longer had to fight the world. I didn't have to hurt others to protect myself. I didn't have to hide being Asian—being Chinese. I could just be me. I was tired of bullying others as a shield. It was empty. Unsustainable. How could I condemn cruelty when I had practiced it myself? That night, I left everything on the beach. A new page was turned.

Chapter 9:
Bonded

2013 was a strange and intoxicating time to be a high schooler. It was my junior year, and suddenly graduation felt close enough to touch, close enough to taste. I was dating my boyfriend Axel, ranked higher in ROTC than I ever expected to be, and for the first time, I didn't feel like I was constantly trying to catch up. We weren't at the bottom anymore, and we weren't awkwardly in the middle either. We have found our footing. We felt established. Confident. Almost untouchable.

Junior year is when the future stops being hypothetical. College applications, recruiters, scholarships, everything starts demanding answers. For me, that future smelled like chlorine and echoed with the hollow sound of an indoor pool. Swimming wasn't just a sport to me; it was the one place where my body felt like it belonged. I loved the quiet pressure of water closing my ears, the discipline of breath control, the calm that came with sinking beneath the surface. People underestimated me constantly, five feet tall, compact, unimposing, until I touched the water.

Then everything changed.

The night of the accident was painfully ordinary. Axel picked me up from my Lifeguard shift, and we decided to grab milk before heading home. I climbed into the passenger seat of his old orange stick-shift truck, the vinyl bench seat cracked from age, the cab smelling faintly of motor oil and fast food. I texted my mom to tell her I was on my way and that we'd stop at the store first.

As we entered the intersection, the light turned yellow. Axel tried to clear it. I remember noticing headlights, too close, too fast. The impact came from my side. There was glass, A violent, metallic scream. The world spun so fast I couldn't tell which way was up. The seatbelt cut into me as the truck rolled, and then suddenly everything stopped. I was hanging upside down, suspended, my head pounding, my thoughts scattered like loose change. I remember thinking about the milk. I remember thinking I needed my calculator.

Someone kicked out the back window. Cold air rushed in. Hands lifted me carefully, voices blurred together, and I was placed on the sidewalk. The concrete felt gritty beneath my palms. My head throbbed. My neck burned. I kept asking for my TI-84 calculator, over and over, because it was expensive, because it was familiar, because my brain clung to something tangible when everything else felt unreal.

Sirens were louder. Red and blue lights smeared across my vision. Gasoline streamed from the truck and ran down the street in a dark ribbon. My mom appeared beside me so quickly it felt impossible, her face pale, her voice shaking as she asked what happened. Tears slid down my face without permission.

They strapped me to a stretcher and loaded me into an ambulance. The ceiling lights were blinding. Every bump sent pain radiating through my skull.

The diagnosis was a severe concussion. Seatbelt burns. Brain inflammation. I was told rest was non-negotiable. No screens. No swimming. No school. My thoughts felt slow and slipping, like my mind was of wet clay. State championships were days away, the meet where college recruiters would be watching.

The door slammed shut without ceremony.

School stopped. My grades froze where they were. I underwent scans and memory tests, sitting in sterile rooms answering questions I knew I should know. Light hurt. Noise hurt. Forgetting hurts the most. I cried when I learned the truck was totaled, every axle snapped. A man at the junkyard later told us he assumed no one survived based on the damage.

Axel also suffered a concussion, but his was mild. I cried anyway, not just because of what I lost, but for how fragile everything suddenly felt. Riding as a passenger terrified me. Turning left still does. Even now, I brace instinctively, waiting for the impact that never comes.

At seventeen, the world feels small. Losing one's future feels like losing the future. My thoughts spiraled endlessly: *Who am I without swimming? What happens now? What am I supposed to become?*

As my brain healed, I slowly returned to ROTC events. I went to junior prom. I pushed through summer training. Somewhere between exhaustion and acceptance, a new decision formed.

On July 3rd, 2013, I enlisted in the United States Marine Corps. It wasn't the dream I had imagined, but it was solid. Purposeful. Something I could hold onto. Axel had already enlisted; he always knew. For me, it was a second choice. But it was still mine. A way to give back to a country that raised me, educated me, and gave me a life I didn't start with.

Senior year arrived like a deep breath before a plunge. Axel and I talked constantly about the future, boot camp, separation, and uncertainty. In our young, determined logic, we made what felt like the most practical decision. We decided to get married. The backlash was immediate and vicious. Family members warned us we were too young, too impulsive. Some of Axel's family turned hostile. What began as disapproval escalated into something uglier: relentless bullying, racism disguised as concern, cruelty disguised as honesty. I had endured racism from classmates before. I was not prepared for it from people who should have been family. They spread rumors, shouted insults at ROTC competitions, and told people I had diseases. Another of Axel's family members screamed slurs without shame. They told Axel they wanted white grandchildren. They made anonymous accusations that nearly cost me my enlistment. I tried to leave Axel more than once—not because I stopped loving him, but because I didn't want to destroy his relationship with his family. Each time, he chose me.

On January 13th, 2014, one day after he turned eighteen, we married quietly at the WWI Museum. My mom and his grandmother watched as we promised ourselves to each other. The date honored my adoption, the symbolic passing of care from my parents to my husband.

When the school found out, we were summoned to the principal's office. We stood there anxiously, wondering why we had both been called in, when a voice echoed from the principal's office into the main office space. "Come in you two."

We slowly walked towards the office, and Mr. Kevin came into view behind his desk. I was already bracing myself for the worst. Axel, I believe, had sweat forming on his forehead. We stood on the opposite side of his desk, our hands nowhere near each other, like two strangers summoned to discuss something we had no part in.

He looked at us for a moment and said, "The reason I brought you both in here was" He paused, probably to catch his breath. To us, it felt intentional, as though he wanted the silence to settle before bringing down the hammer.

Then he continued, "I wanted to tell you both congratulations. It doesn't seem like the logical thing to do, or the most popular, but once you leave these halls, you are adults. The choice you both made to sign a piece of paper and give your lives for this country, well, it's only fitting it's done with the person you choose to love next to you."

His words still touch my heart to this day. I nearly cried. He came out from around the desk, shook Axel's hand, and gave me the warmest, most fatherly hug. Mr. Kevin then said, "I look forward to handing both of you your diplomas this spring. We are all rooting for you and are honored to know you."

We both thanked him sincerely, a phrase we would repeat often in the months ahead as people congratulated us. As we left the office, we looked at one another, newly bolstered with confidence, reassured that we had made the right decision.

As the months passed and the news of our marriage quickly became old, I still felt an overwhelming urge to leave and begin my life in the Marines. The emotional exhaustion caused by some of Axel's family members had drained me to my core. The final straw came at our last competition before heading to nationals once more.

I was standing in the hallway, preparing for the academic test, when I heard them speaking to another cadet's parent. They complained about me, repeating the same criticisms they always had. Then I heard something new. They said I did not deserve their family's last name, or my now-husband's. It was a name earned, not given, unlike the Marines, which they claimed I did not deserve to join either.

In that moment, I broke. I ran down the hallway in the opposite direction, desperate to find somewhere quiet. Axel noticed I was missing and came looking for me. He found me huddled in a corner, crying. He already assumed it involved family members on his side; it usually did, especially during ROTC competitions.

I told him what they had said. Seeing the depth of pain their disapproval and racist bullying had caused me, Axel made a decision that would change everything. Filled with anger and resolve, he stood up and walked back where his family was standing.

They looked at him, clearly unprepared for what was about to be said. Axel stared at them and uttered words no person wants to hear from their own flesh and blood. "I disown you as family."

They became livid and stormed off, likely to cry, the very thing I was already doing elsewhere because of them. From that moment on, he cut off all contact with them. He never spoke to them again.

I watched him make that choice, stunned that it had come to this. They would never know our children. Never see our lives. Never know any details of their family members' future. Axel reassured me that if they were willing to stoop to a level no family member ever should, then he would meet them there. In that moment, I felt proud to be his wife. I felt protected. I felt that no one would ever hurt me again, not with him standing beside me.

Graduation day came and went, and Axel remained true to his promise. He did not see his family, even then. As the days passed, we finalized preparations for our wedding ceremony, scheduled for June 21, 2014. Everyone who mattered most to us was there. It would be the last time we would see many of them for a while.

The day was filled with love, laughter, and well-wishes for the future. The very next day, we shipped off to Parris Island, South Carolina, for the next thirteen weeks. We would not return until we held the illustrious title of United States Marines.

Looking back on that time now, I feel a complicated sadness for Axel's family. I believe they were trying to tell Axel that getting married so young wasn't a good idea. But in doing so, they caused deep harm, harm they never imagined their words could inflict. After all, they were "just words." They never physically abused me. But words can wound.

Because of their actions, they missed out on years of Axel's life. They didn't even know we had a child until he was six months old. Their hatred toward me eventually boiled over into comments wishing my child had been stillborn, words no one, let alone family, should ever speak or think.

As a mother, I cannot justify their actions. I understand their fears and frustrations surrounding our decision, but I will never condone the way they tormented me in high school or wished harm upon my family, especially my son. That is something I may forgive, but I will never forget.

They chose anger and vengeance in a way that was demoralizing and cruel. That is something they alone must live with.

Abram is the most precious half-Chinese child anyone could ever lay eyes on. He is proud of who he is and embraces every part of himself. The story is not about winning or losing; it is about choices, consequences, and the lasting power of words.

Chapter 10:
Crossroads

Our arrival at boot camp was exactly like you see in the videos. We were rushed off a bus and screamed at to stand on the yellow footprints. We yelled at the top of our already exhausted lungs and did everything that was demanded of us, without question and with as much speed as we could muster.

We filed into the building just beyond the footprints. This was where we would receive our platoon assignments, nametags, uniforms, and all the other tedious items necessary for the coming days. We were also given the chance to call home. Telephones lined the wall, each with a script taped above it. We didn't wait for anyone to answer, and if they did, we were to read quickly and hang up immediately.

I heard my mom in a very groggy voice, "Hello?" She had been expecting the call. I quickly read the script as fast as I could, slammed the phone back on the hook, and quickly exited under the watchful, blaring eyes of the Drill Instructors. At this point, we hadn't even met our assigned Drill Instructors yet. The ones yelling at us were the receiving DIs. After that, we ran a Physical Fitness Test (PFT) to ensure we would pass. Only then were we marched into our squad bay. It was spotless, beds lined perfectly in rows, footlockers placed precisely at the ends. Everything was meticulously arranged.

We were ordered to sit on the floor, crisscross applesauce, hands flat on our knees, fingers spread so there was no space between them. Boot camp days were long. Time didn't exist the way it used to. No one knew the exact date or hour. Everything revolved around training days, what day we were on, and how many remained.

Female recruits were all housed in one battalion: 4th Recruit Training Battalion. The male recruits occupied the other three. I was assigned to Company Oscar, Platoon 4032, with an expected graduation date in September of that same year. Time moved painfully slowly, and I learned early on not to stand out. Never be first. Never be last. Blend into the middle, and you might survive unnoticed.

We were allowed to attend church, which became a sanctuary for many Marines—a brief escape from the constant yelling. For me, it was also a chance to see Axel. Males and females were completely separated unless it was church or a rare passing on the streets. Any small glimpse of one another was enough.

Seeing him meant he was still in training. He hadn't fallen out. There were many ways a recruit could be dropped—injury, failure to qualify, exhaustion. If I saw him each week at church, I knew we were both still standing.

The news of our marriage quickly made its way into the Drill Instructor hut. Axel wasted no time sending me letters. When the DIs noticed they were coming from the 1st Recruit Training Battalion, the questions started immediately. How did I know a recruit from the 1st Battalion? Why was he writing me?

Every response had to be in the third person and begin with "this recruit."

"This recruit knows a 1st Battalion recruit because we are married."

Their jaws dropped.

This was the first time they had encountered a recruit married to another recruit in the same cycle. They repeated it back to me in disbelief.

"You are married to a 1st Battalion recruit?"

"Aye, Ma'am."

That was the beginning of a mistake waiting to happen.

They contacted the Drill Instructor hut of the 1st Battalion, narrowing it down by company and platoon. Eventually, the phone rang loudly in Axel's squad bay. A Drill Instructor answered, listened, then burst into laughter.

They stepped out of the duty hut and yelled, "Who is the recruit married to another recruit in the 4th Battalion?"

Silence.

Axel stared straight ahead, knowing exactly who they were looking for. When asked again, he finally answered, "This recruit."

The DIs swarmed him like hungry animals. Sweat dripped down his neck as they mocked him.

"Oh really? You thought you were good enough to be married and be a recruit?"

The DI on the phone hung up and said, "Recruit, this is interesting. Don't piss us off. We have leverage."

They dispersed, leaving Axel shaken but relieved. From that moment on, we knew we had to be flawless. They were watching.

I stayed focused on survival. There was no time for newlywed love. Sometimes it felt intentional, the way we'd pass each other—but we never acknowledged it. A glance was all we allowed. As training progressed, graduation finally felt imminent. We were ready to earn the title. We were ready to leave the island.

Boot camp brought together women from every background imaginable. There were more Asians in my squad bay than I had ever seen in my entire school life—many of them Chinese. More Chinese than me. For the first time, my skin color and eyes weren't the focus. We were all equally considered trash until proven otherwise.

Before the final event, we endured gas chamber qualification, rifle qualification, Marine Corps Martial Arts Program (MCMAP), and countless other evolutions. One day, we trained with pugil sticks— giant Q-tips designed for combat simulation.

The Drill Instructors made a bet: whoever knocked their opponent's mouthpiece out would earn a phone call home.

I loved a challenge. And I despised my opponent.

We fought hard. I sensed her exhaustion and pushed harder, fueled by adrenaline. I struck repeatedly until she dropped to her knees. When her mouthpiece finally flew out after a blow to the back of her helmet, the referee called time—but I didn't hear it. They had to physically pull me off her.

"Coleman," my Senior Drill Instructor shouted, "you earned yourself a phone call home."

That night, I dialed my mom's number from the duty hut. I barely remembered it. When she answered, unsure and sleepy, I said, "Hi mom."

Her voice squealed with joy.

That was the only time I spoke to her until Family Day

Then came the Crucible—54 hours, 48 miles of hiking, eight brutal obstacles, simulated casualties, sleep deprivation, and three MREs meant to sustain us the entire time. No candy. None.

The final march was nine miles to the Iwo Jima Memorial. We stood at attention, soaked in sweat, legs trembling. Locking our knees would've meant collapse.

One by one, Drill Instructors placed the Eagle, Globe, and Anchor into our open palms.

"Congratulations, Marine."

A single tear fell from my eye. A photographer captured that moment, which was later displayed on a wall somewhere. Proof of the day I became a Marine. Afterward, we marched with pride toward our final chow hall meal. The warrior breakfast. Only one week remained.

I finally felt like somebody. I was meant for more. The past no longer defined me. I had climbed the mountain, unaware that an even greater one waited ahead.

After boot camp, we continued on to our next phase of training. I was sent to North Carolina for Military Occupational Specialty School (MOS), where I would learn my job before heading to the fleet. Soon after, I received my orders to Camp Pendleton, California. I was ecstatic; this was only miles away from my older sister, Brooke, who had lived there since her twenties. For the first time, I could taste a real sense of independence.

In the MOS school, I excelled. I was appointed platoon leader and received a Meritorious Mast at graduation. Our instructor was also Asian, which brought an unexpected sense of comfort. The Marine Corps, despite its reputation, carried far more diversity than anything I had known growing up. My small hometown paled in comparison to the world now opening in front of me, and I was elated, ready to take on this new life as a Marine.

Life in the fleet, however, came with both victories and struggles. Before Axel could join me in California, he had to complete a year-long MOS school in Pensacola, Florida, as an aviation electrician. Once completed, he would also be stationed at Camp Pendleton. Because we were married, the Marine Corps ensured we were stationed together, though I had to be placed near or on an air station due to his specialty.

Before Axel arrived, I lived as a barracks Marine. Barracks were similar to college dorms, within walking distance of work, the gym, and the chow hall. All Marines E-3 and below shared rooms, while Noncommissioned Officers (E-4 and E-5) had private ones. Anyone E-6 and above received on-base housing. During my time in the barracks, I had three different roommates. Eventually, I moved into an apartment off base to prepare for Axel's arrival.

We lived off base for the remainder of our time at Camp Pendleton. Life settled into a rhythm, physical fitness, long work hours, and monthly 24-hour duty shifts. My section was diverse, yet I was still one of only two Asians in the building. The other wasn't even in my section.

Despite the diversity, I was again a minority. Teasing followed me almost immediately. My very first weekend in California, still unfamiliar with the highways and traffic patterns, I rear-ended another car in bumper-to-bumper traffic while heading toward Los Angeles to visit my sister. My mom and little brother had just driven the car out to me. I was a mess, confused, scared, and unsure where I even was. Because I was a Marine, I had to report the accident to my Platoon Sergeant. I dreaded it.

Within hours, the entire section knew. The jokes came fast. Asian not using turn signals, "squinty eyes" jokes, exaggerated accents. They mocked me openly. I laughed along, even though I didn't truly see myself as Asian. I became hyper-aware, careful not just with driving, but with how I existed. I didn't want to do anything that could be framed as "Asian."

They even gave me Asian nicknames in Spanish: "El Atonio" and "La Chinita." It was written off as military banter, something civilians wouldn't understand. I didn't fight it. I laughed, deflected, and absorbed it. I wasn't good at witty comebacks, and pushing back only made things worse. It felt like high school all over again. I was the newest piece on the board.

Being a female Marine came with an entirely different set of challenges—misguided assumptions and unspoken realities that don't need detailing here. It's a silent, ongoing issue. Everyone knows it exists. Few acknowledge it.

I'll say this much: I understand what women before me endured, what women alongside me endured, and what women after me will endure. It is not for the faint of heart. You are powerful beyond measure. Anyone who tries to diminish your worth is not worthy of knowing it.

I was a Marine at work, and I was a Marine at home. Being married, active duty to active duty, adds another layer of difficulty. The Marine Corps isn't just a job—it's a lifestyle drilled into you for thirteen weeks and reinforced daily.

I could compartmentalize. Rank stayed at work. At home, we were just husband and wife. Though Axel and I were different ranks for much of our marriage, it was never something I held over him or felt diminished by.

Still, in my early twenties, I spiraled into an identity crisis. I had never seen my birth certificate until I enlisted. When I finally did, feelings of abandonment crept in—dark, heavy, and unavoidable. I had run from them for years, but now they stood directly in front of me.

What followed—without proper support or care—led to breakdowns. I once thought high school had been rock bottom. In truth, that was only a cliff I somehow hadn't fallen from yet.

With the combination of teasing, casual remarks, and my own insecurities, I often felt like a puzzle no one could solve—not even myself. On one hand, I was hyper-aware of being Asian, often reduced to a stereotype or an "exotic" curiosity. On the other hand, my very identity was questioned. I felt like an object of fascination, something to be conquered by male attention, something exotic to be photographed and studied. It was exhausting. Confusing. Painful.

I started questioning everything about who I was. Why did God allow me to be adopted, only to live through a daily storm of judgment, misunderstanding, and rejection? Why did my birth parents not keep me? Why was I not enough? These questions echoed relentlessly in my mind, each repetition layering more anxiety and anger. Even my husband's offhand comments about my race, though never malicious, fueled the spiral. My self-worth plummeted, leaving me with a tornado of destructive emotions. Sometimes I wanted to lash out, to destroy everything around me: family, friends, co-workers, anyone who existed near my pain.

I realized that the only true cure for the emptiness and lack of understanding I felt would be someone who shared my blood. Someone who I could see as undeniably connected to me. Three years into our marriage, I approached Axel about having a baby.

At first, he laughed. He wasn't ready to give up his independence, his freedom. He tried to make me see the joys we were having, the adventures, the fun, things that would inevitably change if we brought a child into our lives. But my desire wasn't about convenience or fun. It was about identity, legacy, and love. I needed someone to carry a piece of me forward, someone to mirror my essence, someone I could finally see myself in.

Axel eventually agreed, though reluctantly. We tried for months. Each negative test crushed me further. Each month, my hope faded a little more, tears flowing over dreams that seemed increasingly unreachable.

Then came that bright Saturday morning at the end of July, the air crisp with a hint of early fall. California is at its best, 70s, sunny, limitless. Ramirez, my best friend, had stayed the night with her daughter. Axel had already left for work when I remembered the last pregnancy test we had. On a whim, I took it.

The word "pregnant" stared back at me. I was in utter shock and couldn't believe it. I called Ramirez immediately, tears and laughter mixing together. She hugged me tightly, whispering congratulations. "How will you tell Axel?" she asked.

We hatched a plan. Axel had forgotten to pack lunch, so I brought him one, using the opportunity to surprise him. I wrapped the test in a small sandwich bag, placed it in a "dad" coffee cup, and tucked it in his lunch. Ramirez filmed everything.

When Axel opened the gift, at first, he was disgusted. Then comprehension hit, followed by an excited, "Awesome!" The joy was immediate. I couldn't contain myself, and neither could Ramirez. The day became a blur of celebration and relief. My dream—finally within reach—was coming true.

The months passed, and the reality of our child grew clearer with each sonogram. In October 2016, we learned the baby was a boy. We had secretly planned a small gender reveal: a pumpkin painted by my sister—pink for a girl, blue for a boy. The reveal was simple, intimate: Ramirez, her family, Axel's brother, my sister, and me. The pumpkin showed a cheerful blue monkey with "Boy, oh boy!" painted above. Tears and laughter erupted immediately. Abram Daniel was due in April 2017.

We prepared everything meticulously: his room in blue and gray chevron with monkeys, crib, changing table, rocking chair, everything shipped by my mom and assembled over weekends. I would often sit in the rocking chair, singing softly to my unborn child, already dreaming of holding him.

As the due date approached, preeclampsia forced an early arrival. My mom canceled her return flight home, ready to help. Abram arrived 4 weeks early, in late March. The birth was intense—15 minutes, the cord wrapped three times around his neck, his skin purple and blue. When he finally cried, I exhaled a long, heavy sigh of relief. The moment my tiny son was laid on my chest, swaddled and calm, the world around me fell away. All the chaos of nurses, doctors, and even family disappeared. It was just us.

Holding him, feeling the life in my arms, I understood something profound. The pain, the anger, the questions of my past, all of it led to this moment. Abram became my answer, my mirror, my bridge to understanding.

In that instant, I finally felt the empathy and grace to understand my own birth mother. I realized the depth of sacrifice; the courage it takes to give a child a life beyond your own control. Abram's arrival didn't just make me a mother; it healed wounds I hadn't known could be healed.

Each day since, Abram has amazed me. Now nearly nine, he has asked me the questions I once asked about myself, and I answer each one carefully, lovingly, with detail. Holding him, I understand the depth of love, sacrifice, and identity that motherhood brings. The lessons extend beyond him—they reach back to my beginnings, to the mother who brought me into this world, and present to the person I am becoming.

Life after Abram's birth moved fast, almost too fast. There was no gentle easing into motherhood, no long pause to recover emotionally or physically. Axel and I were both Marines, and the reality of duty, schedules, and expectations did not soften just because we had brought a life into the world. Still, everything felt different. Every exhaustion had purpose now. Every sacrifice had a face. Those early months were a blur of sleepless nights, feedings, diaper changes, and learning how to function on minimal rest. I remember watching Abram sleep, his tiny chest rising and falling, and feeling a constant undercurrent of fear mixed with awe. I had never loved anything this fiercely. At the same time, I had never felt so vulnerable. I worried constantly—about his health, about whether I was doing things right, about the kind of world he would grow up in.

Balancing motherhood with military life was not easy. There were days when I felt like I was failing at both. I wanted to be present for my son in every possible way, but I also carried the weight of expectations placed on me as a Marine. There was no room for softness in uniform, no allowance for the emotional toll of motherhood. I learned quickly how to compartmentalize—how to tuck my feelings away until the day was done and I could hold my son again.

Axel did his best to support us, though we were both learning as we went. Marriage, I realized, doesn't pause for parenthood—it is tested by it. We argued, we misunderstood each other, and we grew tired. I can honestly say I tried my best. In marriage, as a wife, along with this new identity of being a mother.

As Abram grew, I became more aware of the world through his eyes. I thought often about identity, his identity, my identity, and how the two were now permanently intertwined. I wondered how I would explain his heritage to him, how I would prepare him for questions and assumptions that would inevitably come. I promised myself that he would never feel ashamed of who he was. He would know where he came from. He would know he was loved without condition.

Motherhood softened parts of me that had once been rigid with anger and pain. It also strengthened parts of me I didn't know existed. I became more patient, more intentional with my words, more aware of how deeply words can wound or heal. I thought back to all the things that had been said to me in my youth, all the moments that shaped my self-doubt, and I made a silent vow to do better for my son.

There were moments when the past tried to resurface—memories of cruelty, rejection, and resentment—but they no longer held the same power. Abram grounded me in the present. He gave my pain context and my survival meaning. I wasn't just living for myself anymore. I was building something bigger than my own hurt.

Looking back now, I see how every stage of my life led me here. The struggles, the losses, the anger, the resilience, they all converged into the woman I became as a mother. Abram didn't erase my past, but he reframed it. He turned my wounds into wisdom and my fear into purpose.

I am still learning. Still growing. Still healing. But now, I do so with my son's hand in mine, knowing that the cycle of pain can end with me—and that love, when chosen intentionally, can change the trajectory of a life.

Chapter 11:
Home

Days filled with love, snuggles, and many bottles and diapers were the highlights of 2017 into 2018. When Abram was only a few months old, Axel left for Okinawa, Japan. Because of the number of aviation Marines, they were rotated to other bases that were low-staffed. Axel had been skipped the first time around due to Abram's birth, but he couldn't be skipped over again. He was gone until spring 2018. It was just Abram and me for those months while Axel was away. We spent many nights alone, truly bonding. That first year, being so scary with sickness spread by daycare, Abram had health issues such as the flu and asthma. His lungs were not fully developed at birth, so he needed breathing treatments and medication to assist in their development. Because he was sick often, I had to fly my mom out on numerous occasions to help while I was at work.

Calling in wasn't something the military could accommodate, and if done too often, it resulted in adverse consequences. The first couple of years being a "single mother," per se, were long and exhausting. I was a Marine by day, a college student by night. I was in the midst of earning my bachelor's in accounting. So, weekdays and weekends were filled with bottles, toddler cartoons, and California tax codes. We made it work together.

During Axel's physical separation, I grew increasingly independent, so much so that it was difficult for us to connect both literally over the computer and emotionally. He was living a life on his own in another country, miles away, and I was living as a full-time Marine, mother, and student. This was when our relationship truly began to take its toll.

While he was away, I kept everything running as smoothly as possible. Our differences, if we had any, were emphasized during this period. We both wanted separate things from the beginning, but we did our best to make it work and grow together. My hunger for knowledge and the drive to continue academically and professionally left him behind. He was content living life day to day without ambitions or pursuits.

This topic of growth was a sore one. I knew my life had a greater purpose, and I couldn't live in the mundane. I had to keep climbing the ladder of success to achieve peak self-actualization. I was still striving for that feeling of truly accomplishing something, whatever that may have been, as a young adult. We often didn't communicate about our feelings and allowed the divide of our own priorities to grow until there was no true pursuit of continuing in the relationship. Between multiple mistakes made and the hurt and betrayal I felt, I chose to leave the relationship I had fought so hard to keep in the beginning. I had simply outgrown myself and who I was in that relationship for over four years. The man I was married to had his own personal battles he was fighting. I had again put my very being into the care of someone who ultimately was not my person.

I was not angry or upset with how our relationship ended. We both had a lot of growing and maturing to do, and while we both thought we could do it together, it turned out that these paths were separate and needed to be walked alone.

Because of the internal battles he was facing, I was left on the outside, wondering what was going on and where I stood in his priorities. He was battling between the family he came from and the family we created. He didn't want to give up either, and the issues that were always there with his family's acceptance of me ultimately won the argument.

His family of origin was higher in priority than the family he created. He cared deeply for where he came from, and I was not able to be a part of that reality. All because of the tone of my skin. It was truly like a Romeo and Juliet story being played out on the big screen. Everyone watched with anticipation to see if love could truly conquer all. Yet, because of people's egos and misguided feelings, no one would win in the end.

As I began my new year in late 2018 after our separation and divorce, I was met with the feeling of defeat and rejection. The comfort of the past was too great and ultimately sacrificed our future. I was left with a feeling of abandonment, for myself, our relationship, and the marriage that we stood together and proclaimed. But from all the tears and heartache, I remembered one thing: only good things are meant to last the tests of time and circumstance. If we were meant to truly be, no obstacle would have been too great had both our priorities been each other and the life we had built.

I was again sitting alone, only this time it was legal on paper. It felt as though I could never truly be free from the captivity of my skin, and I was bound by the idea that I would never measure up.

I vowed to continue caring for Abram as if nothing had changed. Even though the worldly status of his life had shifted, it would not truly change anything. The status of being from a "broken home" would not be the front-page cover of his journey. I wanted him to see the courage and bravery it takes for someone to stand up for oneself and leave an undesirable situation, no matter how convenient it would be to stay. I hoped that he would see that while race and ethnicity would continue to be the antagonist, they didn't dictate the rest of the story.

I worked even harder and longer to fill the gaps left by the events of divorce. I did my very best to keep going, even though my heart had truly been shattered and my very being rejected. I realized in that moment that no matter how much trust and belief I put into others, it would not always be enough. True happiness does not come from outward acceptance.

I didn't see any hope of finding "my person." Frankly, I didn't want to, either. The demise of my relationship had been controlled by something I couldn't change, even if I wanted to. I didn't want to put my heart, and now the heart of my son, into the hands of someone who might claim that the color of our skin didn't define their love, when it had already defined our belonging in a country many hold as sacred. I had lost faith in the idea that people were past racism or judging others by appearances. How could people who knew me from a young age not love me because of my origin? Why were their perceptions, based on their belief that I belonged to a race beneath them, taken as fact? They couldn't fathom offering even an ounce of care. Like they would be shamed by God himself for accepting someone of a different race into their lives.

I could never wrap my mind around how people could be so cruel, even wishing harm on someone who had not yet been born. Like their skin color had no flaws, and they were the dominant race, yet they felt entitled to condemn others. I could've come from the wealthiest and most educated family, and it still would not have been good enough. I have always been good enough. I had always been told to be the bigger person and not to stoop to their level. But how is standing up for myself equated to stooping to their level? Why must others walk through life knowing the road they travel isn't filled with flowers and opportunities, but with criticism and humiliation based on a color they didn't choose? These are all things that I still would not fully comprehend until much later.

While my healing process faltered, I knew Abram saw nothing different than his mama. He looked at me with empathy and love and poured it out to fill our home, building a new foundation.

He was, and still is, a living testament that people are not born racist. The way Abram experiences life makes me believe that he will lift people with his empathy and offer endless compassion. It takes a special kind of person who, without speaking a word, can create happiness simply through a touch or a look. I saw these attributes in my child early on and vowed to protect them with my life if needed. He is an empathetic and kind soul who only wishes the best for everyone. In his eyes, no one deserves to walk a road paved with nails and thorns. He sees people for who they are, not who they are supposed to be or who they are pretending to be.

I became okay with the idea that I was meant to walk this life alone. If I had Abram, it didn't matter who I met. I knew I had created the perfect human being—a culmination of all my deepest desires to be accepted without condition. Everyone longs to find a companion who will always have their back, especially when we falter. I hoped that one day Abram would find someone capable of complementing his unique perspective so that together, they could build communities grounded in the belief that all people are created equal.

Just prior to the divorce, Axel and I had bought a home in Kansas. We had planned for me to leave active service and move to Kansas to not only prepare for life outside of active duty, but to finish my service at a nearby unit. Initially, we had thought the military would be our final chapter, but the unexpected shift in trajectory meant it was time to start anew. I ended up keeping the home we bought together and attempted to finance it solely in my name—a decision that would later become a headache.

During this transitional phase, I put my degree to good use, working as a Revenue Accounting Technician with Marine Corps Community Services (MCCS) in Kansas City, MO. Axel was still in California finishing out his five years of service, one year of which was spent in Florida for training. He would not return to Kansas until the summer of 2019.

Abram and I arrived in Kansas in July 2018. I was working, and Abram's days were filled with all things Papa and Grammy—my parents. They became his appointed daycare while I pieced myself back together. Abram has always been infatuated with my parents, especially my dad. If my dad didn't have a "mini me" before, he certainly did now. Abram followed him everywhere. If my dad moved too quickly backward, Abram would be right there, tripping over him with a smile on his face. They were two peas in a pod, and I had fallen just below my dad in the pyramid of importance. We created a schedule and routine that suited our lives. My little brother moved in with us to help financially as he navigated his own path through young adulthood.

After each workday, I would pick up Abram from my parents' house—a two-minute drive. I lived so close that my dad could bicycle over and catch a football game on my living room TV. If I asked how he got in, he didn't need to say a word. Abram would excitedly announce, "I let Papa in. We're watching the game." This was our life, both during the week and on weekends. We were either at my house or my parents' house. I was content, even though technically I was alone.

Each night, I lay in bed staring at the ceiling before Abram awoke from a nightmare, and I would rub his back until he fell asleep. I often thought about not wanting to be alone, especially in my mid-20s. But I was not ready to let anyone into the sacred space I had created for us.

As the faint spark inside me flickered, I didn't yet realize that this was not the end. My life was about to take an unexpected turn, and all I had to do was give up—give up fighting the waves of rejection, give up wrestling with the constant pain—and simply be. Be in the moment. Be okay with not being okay. Be able to set down the bricks I had been holding so tightly. In the quiet of my solitude, as I sat in the darkness with my head bowed in defeat, I noticed something in the distance.

It was 2019, and the world continued to press on, even when I didn't feel like moving. Abram was busy as ever, growing in leaps and bounds, kindness still worn on his sleeves and pouring out of his little heart. He was the light of my world, and even on my worst days, he could turn darkness into beauty. We were together, living as best we could.

I decided, one last time, to put myself out there. I didn't expect to meet "Mr. Right" at the grocery store, and I wasn't into bars or parties. I always preferred the comforts of home. The idea of asking my parents to babysit at night after caring for Abram all day made the thought even less appealing. So, I added myself to a dating app advertised on Facebook. Red flags waved vigorously, and I welcomed the breeze. I signed up for Zoosk and subscribed to a $20, three-month trial—a luxury I technically couldn't afford. I told myself: if I didn't meet someone within the trial, I was done—officially and forever.

Of course, I was matched with 40–50-year-olds with kids. I cannot with the algorithms of these apps. If you admit you have a child, the app assumes you're middle-aged and want the same. If it didn't work out the first time, odds are I didn't want the same thing, and assuming I was middle-aged was just rude. I stopped on one profile and hearted it. The person messaged me back. We navigated the awkward small talk, skimming layers of shame and regret, until we reached the real reasons we were single. My excuse: my child. His long work hours. I had to take deep breaths to not seem desperate, holding my replies to maintain a cool, calm, collected façade.

At least, that was the plan. In reality, I blurted out my entire life story, ending with a smiley face, half-expecting him to think I was a serial killer or that his phone had been stolen. That didn't happen. He replied: "Interesting. Sounds like you've lived quite the life so far." A sweet way to say: that's a lot, but I'm still intrigued.

We continued talking for weeks. One night, craving tacos, I asked if he was available. He had just taken off work for his upcoming birthday and was looking at motorcycles. I suggested he drive from Belton, MO, to Mission, KS, for tacos—not expecting him to do it. But he did. We met at Taco Bell—a safe location, just in case he turned out to be a kidnapper. My brother was at home, adding another layer of security.

The plan got better when I realized I'd left my wallet at home. He pulled out his and paid for the tacos—my first test, which he passed. We took the tacos to my house and ate them while getting to know each other. My brother came upstairs occasionally but didn't interfere.

After dinner, he hinted he needed to leave. He left but promptly messaged me the next day: he had never driven 30 minutes to eat a 12-pack of tacos at a woman's house and then leave, especially with a Taco Bell closer to home. I laughed and said, "I hope you enjoyed the company and it was worth the drive." He replied: "It was nice, and yes, worth the drive."

We continued talking, and I eventually introduced him to Abram. They bonded immediately. Evan, having grown up in a family of 11, was naturally attuned to children. He didn't even have my cell number yet when we exchanged it in May, after his subscription ended. By this point, I had left MCCS and was working at the University of Kansas Health Systems as an Administrative Assistant to Nurse Managers—a job suggested by my brother.

I was still hesitant to fall in love, especially fearing how his family would react to my being divorced and Asian—a fear only those who have walked in my shoes could understand. I met his family at his niece's birthday party in mid-June. He had met my parents around Mother's Day. I was terrified but tried to separate past experiences and give his family the benefit of the doubt. As it turned out, they were welcoming and nonjudgmental. Abram played naturally with his niece and nephews. It was comforting to see that the world could be warm and accepting.

As time went on, it became clear we were falling in love. I repeatedly asked if he truly knew what he was doing. Even now, nearly five years into our marriage, I still ask. He always says without hesitation: "If I didn't want to be in it, I wouldn't be doing it." We discussed our future: settling down, marrying, and having children. His busy work hours had led to failed relationships before, but I came from the Marines and understood the demands. I wanted a partner who would do life together—not someone who only wanted fun, but who would tackle the hard stuff too. I wanted someone Abram could look up to, someone strong and capable, whose home was a refuge no matter the chaos outside.

Ultimately, I wanted someone who would love us without hesitation. I looked at him and asked, "Are you capable of loving someone so broken, with so many flaws? Can you stand against anyone for me, unconditionally, without my skin color becoming an issue?" His response, almost vulnerable, was exactly what I needed: "If I didn't love you and Abram, I wouldn't be here. When I'm alone in my room, all I can think about is being with you two. Since I met you, I've seen what it's like to live alone. I'd rather live this life here, with you and Abram."

That was all I ever wanted—to know I was chosen first. In that moment, I realized that without struggle or force, I had found the one I wanted to spend the rest of my life with. He would always be there. He would stand for our family, make our marriage and our children a priority, and never fear rejecting anyone if it was necessary for us. With Evan, there was never a conflict between his family and us—we were fully accepted.

Looking back at 2019, through the hills and valleys, I could not have imagined how it would unfold. I never expected my life to end and continue in the form of someone quiet, steady, and willing to be whatever we needed. Evan didn't enter like a hurricane; he entered like a calm harbor. He changed his life to be in ours. Fairytales of Prince Charming and castles are myths—but happily ever after exists, created in the chaos and mess of life. It emerges in small, seemingly insignificant moments, shaping the memories you hold most dear.

Chapter 12:
Player 4 Loading

It was the beginning of 2020, the year of the Coronavirus pandemic. Where the world seemed to pause, standing still, awaiting in anticipation of a silent and deadly killer. At the same time, my own life felt suspended in uncertainty. I had just sold the home that I bought only two years prior because I couldn't get it fully in my name. What once felt like security suddenly became temporary.

We packed our entire home and placed everything into storage, where it would sit untouched until the day came when we could reunite with it at its new destination. Whatever that future was supposed to look like. Until then, we moved in with my parents. They had the extra space, and logically it made sense. Especially since they were still our weekday babysitters. Do parents really think they can get rid of us at eighteen? They shouldn't, because that's often when the need for them truly begins.

Evan and I had been dating for almost a year, and we had started to seriously look toward our future. We talked, sometimes subtly, sometimes not, about what the future might include. A ring? A marriage? At least those were not so subtle hints I sprinkled generously into our conversations and time together. He was not going to pretend he didn't see them. I had made up my mind, very rationally, that he is my person. Abram had already accepted Evan as a constant in his life and didn't know any different.

As the pandemic halted the world, we kept moving forward, taking everything one day at a time. Eventually, we found ourselves looking at rental homes. While staying with my parents had been comforting and supportive, it couldn't last forever. Independence was necessary again. Still, I wasn't willing to move into a home together without commitment. I wasn't going to put all my eggs into that basket without something solid to hold them.

It was Labor Day of 2020. We had plans to celebrate the holiday at Evan's parents' house. That morning, I was already short-fused, rushing everyone along so we wouldn't be late. Evan had also agreed to make enough pasta salad to feed the twenty-plus people attending. I hate being late. A Marine who arrives fifteen minutes early is already thirty minutes late.

Evan told me to relax and enjoy the morning. He went down and was preparing breakfast. I took a quick shower trying, trying to calm myself while mentally calculating how little time we had. When I came downstairs, breakfast was already on the table. Sweet? Yes. Helpful? Not on that particular day. Also, why was my boyfriend making breakfast in my parents' kitchen? Had he lost his mind?

I ate quickly and with purpose, then reminded him we needed to leave. I sat on the living room couch waiting for him to finish up when he called Abram upstairs. I remember thinking, I really hope this is productive, asking a three-year-old to help with whatever is happening.

Abram came down the stairs holding a single red rose. He handed it to me with a huge smile. I asked him where it came from.

"The bathroom," he said proudly.

A pleasant place to discover a rose.

I thanked him, gave him a squeeze, and put the rose in a vase with water—still calling out that it was time to go. Abram and I headed out to the car. I sat in the passenger seat while Evan stayed behind, as usual, to buckle Abram into his car seat.

Then Abram came walking around the front of the car holding a small silver box.

My irritation started creeping in. No one seemed to understand the urgency I was feeling. Abram handed me the box and immediately walked back to his side of the car. I opened it and saw that it was empty.

"What is this?" I asked out loud.

I turned towards Evan. He was kneeling near the floorboard, visibly flustered. I asked again, "What is this, Evan?"

He looked up, swallowed hard, and lifted his hands as if he had just picked something up. In a quiet, nervous voice, he asked, "Will you marry me?"

I looked down at the ring and took a moment to process everything. This was not how I had planned it. Not even close. But I smiled, took a breath, closed my eyes, and said, "Yes."

After a short pause, I added, "Now, would you please get in the car so we can go?"

As he buckled Abram in and slid into the driver's seat, Evan said, "It's your fault."

I stared at him. "What's my fault?"

He sighed and explained how he had planned to propose over breakfast with the rose already waiting for me, but my sister had hidden it the day before. He didn't know where she put it, and she was still asleep. That's how the rose ended up in the bathroom. Then I rushed everyone out the door, and since there were already plans awaiting our arrival, he couldn't show up without having already asked me.

"So," he concluded, "it's your fault it wasn't romantic."

I laughed so hard it surprised even me.

"Well," I said, "this will make a great story someday when our kids ask how you proposed."

We arrived at his parents' house on time, pasta salad in hand, only to be greeted by cupcakes shaped like an engagement ring with the words She said yes written in the center. Suddenly, everything made sense. I made Evan reenact the proposal for photos—because there had been no cameras the first time. In true fashion and perfect representation of our relationship, we were officially engaged. I still roll my eyes thinking about how it must have looked from the outside.

Three days after our engagement, the excitement was still settling in when Evan sent me a screenshot of the medical test results. They were from scans related to a shoulder injury he had suffered at work nearly a year earlier. He had been doing physical therapy consistently, but the pain never improved. An X-ray showed nothing. An MRI showed something unclear. An MRI with contrast showed something else. That led to a biopsy.

And then, nothing.

No phone call. No explanation. No warning

With the help of technology and a patient portal, Evan saw the results before a doctor ever spoke to him. He texted me saying he shouldn't have Googled what it meant. When he called, his voice was shaky, and I could hear him trying not to cry. He told me he wasn't going to tell anyone.

I stopped him mid-sentence.

If this was real—and everything in my gut said it was—he couldn't carry it alone. I told him the first people who needed to know were his parents. He went quiet for a moment and then agreed.

The next day, Evan went to his physical therapy appointment and showed his doctor the results on his phone. The doctor barely hesitated before saying, "Yes, that is cancer—and no, we can't treat you anymore." As the doctor continued talking, explaining the next steps and referrals, Evan barely heard a word. Everything after that sentence faded into noise.

After that appointment, he called me. I asked how it went, even though I already knew. He told me he was on his way to his parents' house. I could hear the tears he was trying to hold back, and I knew—brave as he was—he couldn't do this alone.

I told him I was on my way.

When I arrived, Evan was sitting on the couch next to his parents. He had already called ahead to make sure they were home. His mom, a nurse, immediately went into problem-solving mode, reaching out to contacts to get him seen as quickly as possible. Within days, Evan had an appointment to discuss a treatment plan.

By the Friday after Labor Day, he started chemotherapy.

Evan was diagnosed with Stage II Hodgkin's Lymphoma.

Somehow, amid all of that, we were also planning a wedding.

Life quickly became centered around his treatment schedule and protecting his health during the height of COVID-19. Chemo left him immunocompromised, so staying healthy wasn't optional—it was critical. Anyone who planned to be around him needed flu and Covid vaccines. Even at his own sister's wedding, Evan wore a mask and kept his distance from guests.

I picked up extra weekend shifts to help cover expenses when he couldn't work. At one point, I worked thirteen days straight, taking a single day off in between. On treatment days, I would drive to the Cancer Center and wait in the car. Due to Covid precautions, family members weren't allowed inside. His mom would drive him there, and I would take him home afterward. Treatments often lasted until eight o'clock at night. This became our routine for months.

By the end of December, Evan finished chemotherapy and was approved for radiation. During follow-up scans, doctors discovered a seven-centimeter tumor in his chest—something he hadn't even known was there. Four additional lymph nodes were also affected, though they had started shrinking with chemo before being formally identified.

Evan's biggest goal throughout everything was not to make a fuss. He didn't want attention. He didn't want to be treated like a patient. He wanted normalcy.

As a gift to him, I scheduled engagement photos in September, just before chemo began. I wanted him to have something untouched by illness—something that reflected who he was before treatment took its toll.

As the months passed, my main focus was on Evan and his care. I protected his treatment weekends, kept stress away from him, and tried to make life feel as normal as possible. Wedding planning became his escape. He loved touring venues and especially enjoyed cake tastings and food selections. Holidays were hard—his appetite was almost nonexistent—but he still showed up in whatever way he could.

I never once questioned being by his side. I never thought it was unfair. He was my person. He needed me, and I was more than willing to be whatever he needed.

The moment that solidified everything for me, the moment I knew I was fully in, was the day he asked me to shave his head.

His hair had started falling out in clumps, collecting on his pillow. He didn't want to go to a salon. He was embarrassed, protective, and vulnerable in a way I hadn't seen before. So he sat on a dining room chair in the kitchen while I shaved what little hair remained.

With every pass of the Clippers, I watched his reflection in the microwave. I kept my face neutral, pretending not to notice the way his expression changed. I watched a man who had never asked for help, who had served eight years in the United States Army, including a tour in Iraq, slowly become a shell of himself.

Cancer doesn't leave when treatment ends. Even remission carries scars.

Even though they may be in remission and get to ring the bell if there is one, it still leaves a lasting impression on their lives. Evan is nervous to go to doctor's visits; he hates having to have his blood drawn, and he hates having to do scans. Anything that reminds him of that timeframe is tucked away and not seen by the outside world. Any pictures of him during that time, I do have but they are not in permanent frames. They do not take residence in our home.

In April 2021, Evan finished radiation. He went every weekday from January through April, choosing a longer radiation schedule to avoid another round of chemo. And then suddenly, it was May.

Our wedding month.

During treatment, Evan wasn't allowed to drink sugary or caffeinated beverages. This was devastating to a man whose love for Cherry Pepsi bordered on obsession. Not only could he not have it, but he worried he might never want it again. So, for his groom's cake, I surprised him with a three-dimensional replica of a Cherry Pepsi can. Sitting on top was a miniature Evan—complete with his full facial hair glory—holding a tiny Cherry Pepsi. It was one of the few moments where he didn't know whether to laugh, cry, or hide.

Every vendor we chose was a local business. We wanted our money to go directly back into the community—especially those affected by Covid. Many of our decorations were ordered from small Etsy shops, and our guest favors were hot chocolate bombs in different flavors. The entire day was filled with thoughtful details, all reflecting Evan's resilience and quiet strength.

Our wedding day brought some of the hardest rain that spring had seen. It poured relentlessly. Guests returned home to flooded basements. But the rain wasn't going to ruin our parade. We danced in it. The weather became just another part of our story.

Surrounded by our closest family and friends, we celebrated not just our marriage, but everything it had taken to get there. It was a day of gratitude, relief, and love. Evan stood there—healthy, present, and smiling—and that alone made it perfect.

A few days later, we left for our honeymoon in Honolulu, Hawaii. Five days of tropical air, ocean breezes, pineapples, and peace. It felt like a victory lap. We swam with sea turtles, toured the island, and visited the Pearl Harbor Memorial. It wasn't just a honeymoon—it was a celebration of survival. A quiet acknowledgment of how close we had come to losing everything, and how lucky we were to still be standing together.

We missed Abram terribly while we were gone. Before leaving, we had prepared little surprise bags for him—one for each day—with notes, toys, and treats to remind him that he wasn't forgotten. When we returned home, he was waiting for us, and our family felt complete again.

We handed out souvenirs as a thank-you to everyone who had helped us—those who watched Abram, cared for the house, or supported us in ways big and small. Life finally felt settled. For the first time in a long time, we could breathe. And that's when we began thinking about expanding our family.

We knew early on that chemo and radiation meant there was only a fifty-fifty chance Evan would be able to help conceive. It was something we discussed honestly. Evan had already accepted that Abram might be our only child. We agreed we wouldn't pursue IVF or fertility treatments. If it was meant to happen, it would.

Month after month, I stared at negative tests and single pink lines. I tracked cycles. I used ovulation sticks. I cried on bathroom floors. I told myself stories about acceptance and letting go—none of which stuck. The pressure became unbearable, and the hope slowly turned into quiet grief.

Eventually, I told Evan I was done trying. I threw away the last box of pregnancy tests. I needed to stop breaking my own heart.

People told me to relax. That it could take a year. That it would happen when it happened. Those words—though well-intended—felt impossible to hear from the other side of the journey. For anyone who has struggled to conceive, even briefly, you know the ache. It doesn't matter how long it's been. Wanting something so deeply and feeling powerless to make it happen changes you.

I didn't experience infertility the way so many women do—but I felt a piece of the pain. And to those walking that path longer than I did: you are seen. You are allowed to feel everything. Anger, grief, jealousy, hope, exhaustion. Give yourself the grace you'd give anyone else.

In the fall of 2021, our lease was ending, and we faced another major decision: renew or buy. The cost was nearly the same, and the housing market had exploded. Houses sold almost as quickly as they were listed—and often for far more than the asking price.

The search was exhausting. Time was not on our side.

Then we found the one.

We wrote a heartfelt letter to the seller, hoping it would set us apart. Somehow, it worked. The house was ours. In December 2021, we moved in with the help of family and the usual payment of pizza and drinks.

True to form, I stayed up for twenty-four hours straight unpacking. By morning, the house looked finished—decor on the walls, furniture in place, boxes stacked neatly in the garage. When Evan and Abram woke up and walked down the hallway, their faces said everything.

The house was perfect.

And yet, buried deep in my heart, the desire to become a mother again still lingered.

By early 2022, I had convinced myself that motherhood beyond Abram simply wasn't meant for me. I had said the words out loud enough times that I almost believed them. Almost. Still, there was a quiet ache that never fully went away—something I learned to tuck into the background while focusing on the life we had rebuilt.

It was March 2022. A gray, cold weekday, soaked in rain much like our wedding day had been. I was at work, going about my routine, when I decided to make a quick stop at urgent care. I didn't have an appointment with my regular doctor, and whatever I was experiencing wasn't serious enough for the emergency room. I just wanted reassurance.

The knock on the door came, and she walked in. I sat there, almost half-grinning, knowing the test had come back negative. She stood in front of me, placed her hand gently on my leg, and with a small smile said, "Autumn, you are pregnant."

I immediately started to cry. "No," I said, shaking my head. "You can't be right. No. Did you accidentally switch my stuff with someone else's?"

She gave me a look—the kind that suggested I might be pushing it by questioning her abilities as a medical professional. I smiled weakly. "I'm sorry. I just… I can't believe it." I covered my eyes with my hands and sobbed into them. Then I added, "We had been trying for a while, and it was always a 50/50 chance after my husband's cancer."

She stood there, smiling and nodding, assuring me without words that she wasn't lying and this wasn't a mistake. I finally composed myself, thanked her, and left the room with adrenaline racing through my body.

I made my way back to my office and immediately began planning how I was going to tell Evan. After work, I needed to grab Abram and rush home because we were meeting Evan's brother and sister-in-law for dinner. I decided to take advantage of Target's "pick up" service— one of the few genuinely good things to come out of Covid. I bought a card that read "Congratulations. You did it." and a baby remote-control toy. As Abram sat with me while I put the gift bag together and signed the card, I added, "Player 4 loading…" Abram was hysterically laughing in the backseat, finding it hilarious that I was giving Evan a "baby toy."

On the drive home, still in the pouring rain, I called my sister-in-law and asked for her help. I needed her to videotape the surprise. She agreed, and when we arrived, she was already inside with Evan, waiting. She held her phone in a way that wouldn't raise suspicion as I handed him the gift bag. He immediately assumed it was for his birthday in April and grew visibly awkward, once again placed in the spotlight—apparently, our wedding had been enough attention for one lifetime.

He glanced at the card and jokingly skipped past it, then picked up the baby Xbox controller and started making comments about how it wouldn't even hook up to the system. I rolled my eyes and told him to read the card. Still embarrassed, he opened it and read what I had written. He looked up at me as it clicked.

"We did it?" he asked.

I nodded. He hugged me and said, "Yay, I did it." We all laughed and headed out for dinner. Abram, still blissfully unaware of the full meaning of it all, was giddy and laughing along. We wouldn't explain it to him until later—it was still early, after all.

So, our journey began once again.

Ah yes—the joys of pregnancy. The basking glow. The miracle of life growing inside you. The congratulations, the cheers, the magical experience. Birds chirping sweet melodies as the sun rises, woodland creatures awakening to greet the day.

Yeah… no.

I don't know how some women experience pregnancy like Cinderella waking up or Snow White singing while she cleans. My memories of pregnancy did not include any sort of glow—unless you count the light reflecting off stretch marks so large it looked like I had been mauled by a ferocious tiger. There were the hormones that made me want to eat and vomit simultaneously. The exhaustion that felt like I'd just completed a triathlon. Oh yes, very "magical."

When I was pregnant with Abram, I had apparently forgotten what pregnancy was actually like. No exaggeration—my body completely erased the memory. This time, it all came rushing back, as if someone in my brain found missing files shoved to the back of a filing cabinet and dumped them straight into short-term memory. All of this happened while I stood there trying to swallow a prenatal vitamin the size of a small weapon—made of some mysterious ingredient that disintegrates the second it touches moisture. Pregnancy is amazing and beautiful, truly… and I still don't understand why we keep wanting to do it.

As we approached finding out the baby's gender, Evan, Abram, and I all wanted it to be a boy. It felt easier—an easier transition, another little brother for Abram. But deep in my gut, I had this unmistakable feeling it was a girl. Still, as usual, I doubted myself and leaned into believing it was a boy.

The results were sealed in an envelope and given to my best friend, Cydney, who would reveal the gender at our party. It was August, and the anticipation was unbearable. The immediate family gathered for a "Lashes or Staches" party, beautifully organized and themed. The colors—light pink and navy blue, perfectly echoed our wedding palette. Everything felt just right.

Right before the reveal, the balloon arch stretched from pillar to pillar, gently swaying in the breeze. Suddenly, the largest light-pink balloon popped without warning. Everyone jumped, then laughed, assuming it was a sign. Cydney handed us the tubes filled with confetti.

Evan and I stood together, counted down, and twisted. Pink. A girl.

As the confetti floated down, our faces were frozen in shock while everyone cheered. Abram immediately burst into tears and ran off. We had unintentionally hyped him up in one direction, and my heart sank. Embarrassed, he hid behind a nearby tree. While people took photos around us, I slipped away to find him.

He was leaning against the trunk, hands covering his eyes. I knelt beside him and waited quietly until he sensed I was there. He looked up, lowered his hands, and sighed, his little body limp against the tree.

"Can you return it to the baby store and get a boy?" he asked.

I tried desperately not to laugh at his innocence. "No, sweetheart," I said gently. "It doesn't work that way." I sat beside him and pulled him closer. "I'm sorry Mommy and Daddy made you think it was a boy. We didn't mean to hurt your feelings."

He looked at me with tear-stained eyes. When I told him we had wanted a boy too, his expression softened, relieved that he wasn't alone. "But," I added, "I think having a little girl is going to be amazing."

He looked at me, unsure. "It will?"

"Oh yes," I said. "Because you'll always be my baby boy, and she'll be my baby girl—both loved more than anything."

He closed his eyes and let out a deep breath. Together, we returned to help clean up. Evan looked at me, silently asking if Abram was okay. I gave him a look that said, He will be.

When we got home, I finally started looking up girl items on Amazon. Until then, I hadn't bought a thing; I didn't want to be wrong. Her room would be pink and floral. The very next day, a package appeared on the porch, earlier than expected. Evan watched as I opened it. Inside was a soft white blanket with numbers one through ten, days, weeks, months stitched along the bottom—and in the corner, the sweetest little panda.

I looked up at Evan, tears forming (hormones, obviously). "Do you like it?" he asked.

"I love it," I said. "Did you get this?"

"Yes," he replied. "As soon as we found out it was a girl. I made sure it arrived this weekend."

It was the perfect backdrop for monthly milestone photos. Everything suddenly felt real, like it was falling into place. Though I was still hesitant, I found myself truly anticipating her arrival.

Chapter 13:
Love Multiplied

November of 2022 what a month to be born.

I went to my 37-week checkup as planned, feeling overly large and waddling back and forth like a penguin. I crossed the hospital using all the connecting bridges to get to my appointment from where my office was located. As the nurse checked my vitals, like always, she looked concerned. She decided to check them again. Still, concerned. She said that we would check them once more in the middle of the visit and that my OBGYN would be in shortly.

I started to get nervous, truthfully, mentally prepared myself for them to tell me I was not going to be leaving without birthing this child.

My OBGYN made her appearance and decided to check my vitals herself. Sure enough—high blood pressure. She looked at me and said, "Are you ready? Because you look at it." I replied, "I truthfully am over it and have been since the 30-week mark." She smiled and said, "Well, you're technically full term, and seeing as you haven't moved much and your blood pressure is quite high, let's get you triaged to Mother/Baby."

Yes. Thank you, Jesus.

I didn't care what day of the month it was, even though she was supposed to be born on 11/26/22. They called Mother/Baby and told them to expect my arrival. I was wheeled over in a wheelchair and hooked up to the monitors. Lying there, I continued to have three separate high blood-pressure readings. The staff confirmed what I already knew—I was not going to be leaving without having a baby.

They moved me into a delivery room and again hooked me to monitors. I was prepped for medication to induce labor. I called Evan and told him it was time. We had already planned for my parents to take care of Abram and the animals while we were away. It just so happened that my mom was in California, and my poor father and little sister took on the duties that had been set up for her.

My dad brought Evan to the hospital since my car was already there from work, and my little sister picked up Abram and took care of him at the house. My dad sat in the hospital chair in the corner, looking around the room. He never liked being in hospitals, even for happy occasions. Evan occupied the recliner, and I was front and center in the bed.

I looked at my dad and said, "Dad, you can leave if you want to. You don't have to stay."

He looked at me and said, "Well, what did your mom do the first time? Aren't I supposed to be here?"

I laughed immediately and said, "Dad, you don't want to be here. You come after the baby is born. I'll be fine, and Evan is here. Go home and get some sleep. These things take time."

He jumped up and said, "Thank God!" He didn't want to be there either for what was about to come next

As time ticked on, I told Evan to get comfortable and try to sleep, because when it was time, it would be time—and this wasn't something we could plan down to the hour. He lay down and tried to rest. I, on the other hand, was already uncomfortable and had been awake since 4 a.m. that morning. By now, it was midnight, and progress was steady but slow.

The nurse came in periodically to check on me and gave me a warning: if I was going to receive the epidural, it needed to be done now. Any further, and it would be too late. I decided to get it done. Evan had just fallen asleep and was then told to move, as the space where he had been sitting became the sterile area.

I got the epidural and continued through the laboring process. I tried to get a few minutes of rest, but as the clock ticked on, sleep was not going to happen for me. By early morning, approaching 6 a.m., the doctor came in and decided to go ahead and break my water. After that, it was time to deliver quickly.

Evan, looking exhausted and nervous, held my hand as we prepared for her birth. I took one last look at him and said, "Whatever you do, do not pass out." He nervously grinned, trying not to.

Our baby girl arrived within a few pushes, weighing 7 pounds 4 ounces—an ounce smaller than Abram. Her length was 19 and 1/8 inches, while Abram had been 19 and 1/2 inches. Up to this point, I had worried about what it would feel like to be a mother again. I didn't want Abram to feel replaced. He was my first, and I didn't know what emotions would come with a second. I had asked my mom what it was like to have a second child. She said, "It is different than your first, but feels like it's the first time. I love you all equally and differently. Each love is special and unique." I had always thought that couldn't be true. There had to be a favorite. How could someone love two children the same? But as I held my daughter for the first time, I understood—love could be both equal and different.

As they placed my daughter on my chest, memories of Abram's birth flooded back. The room became a blur; everyone seemed slower as they continued their tasks. I stared at that little girl and knew in that moment that yes, you can love another human as much as the first, and this love is still different. Our connection was something I could never fully put into words. All my fears and worries about being a "girl mom" vanished instantly. Her little eyes focused on mine. I started to cry and whispered, "Mommy loves you with everything in me. I promise, you will do great things someday." Everything was perfect. Once again, God had blessed me with our sweet girl—Ellie Louisa, "God's promise," born on Veteran's Day.

When Abram came to meet her, he walked into the room quietly and slowly. He looked at Ellie, and his eyes filled with tears. I asked if he was okay. He said, "I love her so much. I'm glad she isn't a boy." He didn't want to hold her yet, nervous about hurting her. He left and would see her the next day when we arrived home. Abram just wanted to be near her. It took his cousins holding her for him to gain the courage to do it himself.

Finally, he wrapped her in his little arms and held her tight, careful not to drop her. She stared up at him, and he spoke softly, almost reverently, "Hi Ellie. I am your big brother. You are going to be my best friend. I will protect you and love you forever." My heart nearly fell out of my chest watching this moment. I not only saw two people choosing love, but two young souls, innocent and flawless, creating a bond from scratch.

This beautiful moment of interpersonal connection affirmed that human beings are just that, human beings. They are each created uniquely, mixed with a complex DNA of both of their parents.

This beautiful moment of connection affirmed something essential: human beings are human first. Ellie and Abram, though they have different fathers, share the same mother—and to them, that makes them siblings fully, completely. Blood does not define the depth of love or the legitimacy of family. These precious moments happen daily, often unseen, but they shape lives far beyond the snapshot captured on social media.

As time went on, I began reflecting on what it truly meant to be a mother of two. The moment I held Ellie, it was magical—not different than holding a little boy, not better or worse, just different. But the unresolved emotions from my past made recovery from childbirth unbearable at times. I allowed darkness to seep into my being, believing the things I had been told my whole life: that I was either "blessed" for being adopted or an alien who should not have set foot in the U.S. I was hurting—emotionally, mentally, physically. The stubbornness that had always kept me pushing forward felt like it had evaporated. I was left alone in the dark, without the tools to fight.

I had hidden my true aggression, anger, and bitterness for so long, hoping they would drown in my heart. But one night, I couldn't hide it anymore. The house was still, everyone was asleep, and I found myself on the cold kitchen floor, back against the cabinets, head tilted toward the ceiling, trying to catch what little air I could. My body sank into the ground, and I cried silently, afraid to wake anyone. I looked up and whispered to the universe, "I am done. I cannot do this anymore. I don't want to do this anymore." My spirit had always believed things would get better, that each fall meant I could rise again—but this time, it was too much.

During Christmas, I went out for coffee with one of my dearest friends. We sat against a wall on the second floor of their favorite coffeehouse, and our conversation began lightly. But they sensed something was wrong. They asked, "Are you okay?" I wanted to say "yes" and move past it, but I couldn't. The weight of everything I had held inside came crashing out. I began to cry.

I told them that I hated being adopted. I couldn't bear the pressure of it, the expectation that I should feel grateful or "blessed." I felt I would never be worthy enough to live up to that title. They looked at me with confusion and asked, "What do you mean?" I repeated, wiping away tears, "Ever since I could understand my situation, I've tried to forgive, forget, turn the other cheek, live up to expectations—but I can't do it anymore. Everyone tells me I should be grateful my parents chose me, that I got a second chance at life. But I didn't ask for this. I didn't ask to be brought here. I don't want to hurt my parents, but I can't bear the weight anymore. I sometimes wish I had just died, like I should have, because I couldn't survive as a Chinese orphan."

My Friend listened quietly, letting silence fill the space. They took a sip of coffee and said, "Autumn, if not your parents, someone else would've adopted you. You weren't 'chosen' in some special way— you were on a list, along with other children, and it was your turn. There's a greater likelihood you would have ended up in Colorado, where the agency was. Your adoption is not your burden to bear."

Their words hit me like a revelation. All this time, I had believed I had to justify my existence, prove my worth, earn my parents' love through achievements and gratitude. They continued, "You don't owe anyone for your life. Take the garbage people have put on you and throw it in the trash where it belongs. People are taught to hate, to feel uncomfortable around what they don't understand. Honestly, fuck them. Fuck anyone who pushes you to believe you're not worth breathing. You may have been born in China, but that does not define you."

I cried harder, feeling a weight lift. I had feared having a daughter because I couldn't protect her from a world I hadn't yet fully survived. I couldn't shield her from the cruelty, the judgment, the constant pressure to be something she was not. I realized then that I could not teach courage or bravery if I didn't first allow myself to feel safe and worthy.

I admitted to my friend all the times I had tried to end my life— driving off a cliff in California while Abram giggled in the backseat, swallowing an entire bottle of Ibuprofen, and collapsing in my kitchen. Evan had found me that night and insisted I get help. I had been so alone, trying desperately to prove my worth to a world that seemed determined to reject me. I told them, "I just don't want to be alive anymore if this is the life I have to live."

They reached across the table, took my hand, and said, "You are beautiful. You are loved. You are not a burden or a mistake. You were meant for life, not death." Their words were like warm streams pouring over me. They reminded me that I did not owe anyone, that I did not need to carry the weight of the world or justify my existence. The burden of being "chosen" was not mine. The cruelty of others was not my fault.

I felt a release I hadn't known possible. For the first time, I began to understand that life could be something I lived for myself and my children—not for the expectations or judgments of others. I had previously lied to myself and released whatever tensions and anger I had. But in reflection was just riding a roller coaster going forward, then backward continuously on a loop, just surviving.

As I sat with those words, something inside me shifted. I began to see how deeply societal expectations had shaped the way I viewed myself—especially as a woman, an adoptee, and now a mother to a daughter. The pressure to be palatable, grateful, soft, and resilient all at once had carved itself into my bones. I had spent my life trying to meet invisible standards set by people who never stopped to ask how heavy they were.

Becoming a mother to a girl forced me to confront questions I had avoided. How do you raise a daughter in a world that critiques her before she even speaks? How do you teach her to love her body when you were taught to disconnect from your own? How do you protect her spirit without teaching her fear? I realized that my hesitation about having a girl was never about her—it was about me. It was about the unresolved pain I carried and the fear that I would unknowingly pass it on.

I watched Ellie sleep in those early weeks, her chest rising and falling in quiet rhythm, her tiny fingers curling instinctively. She had no idea what the world would demand of her someday. In those moments, I made a silent promise to her: I would do the work. I would not ask her to be brave in ways I refused to be. I would not teach her self-worth through survival alone.

Motherhood the second time around was humbling. With Abram, everything felt urgent—every milestone, every decision, every mistake. With Ellie, I felt slower, more intentional. I understood that perfection was never the goal. Presence was. Love was. Showing up even when I felt broken was enough.

I began therapy again, this time not as a last resort, but as an act of self-respect. I started speaking more honestly, even when my voice shook. I allowed myself to grieve the life I never had, the identity I had been forced to carry, and the little girl inside me who learned too early how to disappear. Healing was not linear. Some days felt victorious; others felt suffocating. But I stayed. I chose to stay.

Evan watched this transformation quietly. He never pushed, never demanded explanations. He held space when I needed silence and stepped in when I needed grounding. There were nights when I cried into his chest, apologizing for being "too much." He would pull me closer and say, "You're not too much. You're human."

Abram, in his own way, became my reminder of hope. He would ask thoughtful questions, wrap his arms around Ellie, and announce proudly that he was her protector. Watching him grow into empathy reaffirmed that love, when modeled honestly, multiplies.

I no longer saw my story as something to overcome or hide. It became something to own. My adoption, my pain, my motherhood— all of it intertwined into a narrative that was mine alone. I didn't need to romanticize it or minimize it. It simply was.

Ellie did not arrive to fix me. She arrived to remind me. To remind me that life is not about earning your place in the world—it's about existing fully in it. And for the first time, I allowed myself to believe that I belonged here too.

In the weeks and months that followed, life settled into a rhythm both familiar and entirely new. Each morning, the house hummed with the sounds of my children stirring—the soft babble of Ellie's coos, Abram's footsteps padding across the floor, the distant whistle of the kettle. There was chaos, yes, but also an unspoken beauty in it, a reminder that life is messy and precious in equal measure.

I began to notice the small moments—the way Ellie's tiny fingers wrapped around mine without hesitation, how Abram would sit quietly beside her, reading aloud from his favorite books, or how Evan, exhausted from work, would kneel on the floor just to make her laugh.

These were not the grand moments captured on social media or celebrated in photos; they were ordinary, unremarkable, yet profoundly significant. They reminded me that love is often found in the quiet persistence of showing up, in gestures so small they almost go unnoticed, and yet leave an imprint on the soul.

There were difficult nights, too. Nights when Ellie wouldn't sleep, and my patience thinned to a whisper. Nights when Abram, despite his maturity, tested boundaries in ways only children can. Nights when I would sit on the floor, cradling both of them in my arms, feeling the weight of responsibility pressing down, and yet simultaneously, the depth of joy that comes from being fully alive in the present.

Through all of this, I continued my inner work. I journaled with honesty, peeling back layers of resentment, self-doubt, and fear. I challenged the old narratives I had carried for so long—about my adoption, my worth, my place in the world. Slowly, the voice that had whispered "you are not enough" began to fade, replaced by one that said, "you are here, you are human, and that is more than enough."

Motherhood became a mirror. Through Abram and Ellie, I saw my own strengths, my blind spots, and the ways my past had shaped my responses. I began to understand the delicate balance between protection and freedom—teaching them to navigate the world safely, yet allowing them the space to stumble, fall, and rise on their own. I realized that part of my role as a mother was to cultivate resilience, not shield them from the challenges of life.

And then there was joy—pure, unfiltered joy. A laugh shared over spilled milk, a tiny hand reaching for mine in the morning light, the wonder in Ellie's eyes as she discovered the world around her. These moments reminded me that even amidst pain, chaos, and uncertainty, life has the capacity to be beautiful.

I also began to reflect more on the broader lessons of my journey. Adoption, identity, systemic injustice, and personal trauma were not just experiences to endure—they were opportunities to grow, to empathize, and to connect with others in meaningful ways. I started to see that my story, while deeply personal, had the power to resonate with others, to inspire dialogue, and to illuminate truths that are often overlooked or silenced.

Most importantly, I learned that acceptance is not a single moment of clarity but a continual practice. Accepting myself, my past, my present circumstances, and my place in the world became a daily commitment. It required patience, self-compassion, and the willingness to confront uncomfortable truths. But with each passing day, I felt more anchored, more present, and more capable of loving myself and my children without reservation.

Life, I realized, is not about perfection or fitting into a prescribed mold. It is about showing up, feeling deeply, and embracing the fullness of your experiences—the joy, the pain, the uncertainty, and the beauty. It is about creating space for growth, for love, and for light to enter even the darkest corners.

As I watched Abram and Ellie play together, their laughter echoing through our home, I felt a profound sense of gratitude. Not for a life without struggle, but for the resilience, love, and connection that had brought us to this point. I understood, finally, that my journey— through adoption, identity, motherhood, and self-discovery—was not a burden but a gift. A gift that had taught me how to fight, how to love, and how to exist fully and unapologetically.

Epilogue

Intricately placed amongst these pages is my pieced-back-together heart, unwavering passion, and innermost being. My journey to self-acceptance was not without fault, nor without my own demise along the way. The intention of my story was to speak life with purpose. Give you a glimpse into the reality of a person thrust into adversity yet destined for greatness. The idea that the most precious of creations is often overlooked amidst the harshest conditions.

Each monumental and uneventful lived experience has taught me the value of life. Walking my path is not meant to replicate the path of another. Each person must have the freedom to lay their own bricks, creating the path that reflects their truest form. I have evolved many times over. I will continue to change, because the life we are given only once is not stagnant.

I have fallen repeatedly and shattered further the pieces that were already broken. I spent years sprinting towards death, disregarding the life I was living. Reflection does not come after the planting, budding, apogee, and disappearance. You are simply pressing rewind and replay repeatedly. True reflection must be fluid. It must be open to the shifting and adaptability of your existence.

Great leaders and world changers may possess leadership qualities from birth, but a true leader doesn't place their faith solely in that concept. They are continual learners, remaining open-minded to the knowledge yet to be attained. There is capability of "natural-born leaders," but commanders are formed through belief. I am unapologetically me.

I dedicate this narrative to my children. May your journey to self-acceptance come with the knowledge of your ancestral past. Please do not follow suit, but take this and forge your own futures. I have learned from my experiences and hope I am creating safe and open environments for you. That I am your safe place. Where you do not have to be anything or anyone. You can simply be. You are my greatest accomplishment. I live because you showed me that death doesn't create change. If I am blessed, it is because I knew you. I was merely the vessel through which you entered this world.

Ellie, may you know how valuable you are. My desire for you is to know that you are equal. You can and will move mountains if you choose to do so. Empowering women builds economies. Know that I love you with every fiber of my being. You have taught me to be kind to myself, to allow myself grace. What I freely offer to so many. I hope you know you were created in God's image, fearfully and wonderfully made. You are clothed in strength and dignity. Do not fear the world. Embrace it with your fire that will illuminate the dark. You will be the greatest version of you that ever walks this earth.

Abram, may you never lose sight of your empathetic heart and emotional intelligence. You will do miraculous things someday. I love you with every fiber of my being. Whatever and wherever your journey takes you, I wish only true happiness for you. You have triumphed through so much. Take time to bask in your victories, as your steadfast belief in God and in people continues to shine light on those around you.

I have always told my children: you are a lake filled to the brim with water. Every choice you make creates a ripple. Will your choices cause rocks to crash into your waters, sinking to the bottom and filling the darkness of your lake with wasted space? Or will your choices produce leaves that fall gently onto the surface, barely touching it, allowing the water to remain undisturbed? The choice is yours.

It is acceptable to have all the feelings you do. It is valid to feel what you feel in circumstances. But the issue arises when those feelings surpass you and are pushed onto those around you. Try not to create rocks in other people's ponds.

I have grown in leaps and bounds, both personally and professionally. I will never be "done," even after I breathe my last. With this narrative now clear, I am able to take strides forward. I will continue laying the foundation of my path, planting Cherry Blossoms along the way, hoping that this brings beauty and light to your chaos, creating space for your own interpretation and meaning.

May you be a Cherry Blossom in a world of thorns. And if the world is overflowing with them, who could truly stand against us?